D0949456

To "Uncle Lew," whose vision and dedicated effort made it possible for millions to discover that PRESSURE COOKING IS PLEASURE COOKING.

Seventh Printing . . . June, 1979

My grateful acknowledgment to the
R. T. French Company, National
Presto Industries, Inc., and the
Thermos Division of King-Seeley
Thermos Company for photographs
used in this book. And a special
thank you to Presto's Home
Economists — Betty Wenstadt and
Jo Anne O'Gara — for their co-
operative efforts in developing and
testing the recipes.

Pressure Cooking is Pleasure Cooking

THE COMPLETE COOKBOOK
FOR PRESSURE COOKERY

By Patricia Phillips

© 1973
The Johnson Press
Eau Claire, Wisconsin

Cooking and meal planning will bring you greater success ... and take you less time ... with your pressure cooker as your aide and this new cookbook as your guide.

Between these covers you will find a wealth of recipes especially developed for your pressure cooker: exciting new recipes, old-fashioned favorites, recipes from countries afar, simple fare to please children, easy ideas for hurried days, company fare for discriminating guests. You can follow these recipes with confidence, for every one has been tested for you by professional home economists.

And together with the recipes are menus to speed weekly planning, tips on being a smart food shopper, food lore, hints and helps, even ideas for impromptu family-only parties.

We hope this book will be a help in your busy life, giving you confidence, knowing that a delicious. dinner is only minutes away.

CONTENTS

LIST OF ILLUSTRATIONS

10 Easy Steps To Make Pressure Cooking a Pleasure

After following these steps faithfully a number of times, you will soon be doing them perfectly . . . automatically.

1. Prepare ingredients following the particular recipe you've chosen from this book. Many meat recipes will call for searing the meat before adding liquid to the cooker.

2. Pour the required amount of liquid into the cooker. Since pressure cooking is cooking food in a steam atmosphere, this liquid is essential.

3. Add foods and seasonings according to the recipe. The recipes in this book are for the 4-qt. cooker; if you have the 6-quart cooker, recipes may be increased by one-half. Never fill your cooker over ⅔ full; this allows for food expansion during cooking.

4. Hold cover to light and look through vent pipe from underside of cover to be sure vent pipe opening is not blocked. Another way is to run a pipe cleaner through the vent pipe.

5. Fit cover on the cooker. With the cooker handle in your left hand and the cover handle in your right, lock the cooker closed.

6. Place the pressure regulator on vent pipe.

7. Set the cooker on the range. Turn burner on high heat to exhaust air from the cooker.

8. *When cooking pressure, 15 pounds, is reached, the pressure regulator begins to rock. Immediately start to count the cooking time specified in capital letters in the recipe. At the same time, lower the heat of the burner, using just enough heat to maintain pressure during cooking. Use an accurate ninute timer for timing cooking. Don't risk overcooking foods; 1 minute of pressure cooking equals 3 minutes regular cooking.*

If the recipe directions say: COOK 0 MINUTES, this means to cook food only until cooking pressure, 15 pounds, is reached, then remove cooker from heat and cool according to recipe.

9. *As soon as the cooking timer rings, reduce pressure as directed in the recipe.*

To "let pressure drop of its own accord," set cooker aside to cool. This usually takes about 5 minutes. This additional time must be reckoned into the total cooking period if you wish to serve your family on the dot.

To "cool cooker at once," place it under cold running water or place it in a pan or sink full of cold water.

10. *After pressure has been completely reduced, first remove pressure regulator, then the cooker cover. Remove food to serving dish. If desired, reheat cooker — without pressure — to thicken gravy or sauce to accompany food.*

SOUPS

Did you know that our American word, supper, comes from "la soupe," the name of the evening meal in provincial France? And what a wonderful supper soup makes when it is chock-full of meat and vegetables, served steaming from your pressure cooker.

Warming, rib-sticking homemade soup is especially welcome on raw, chilly days. Try these generous recipes — there's never a worry about second bowlfuls.

Why not set a certain night of the week as "soup night" and try a different recipe from this collection each week? Prove to yourself and your family that soup makes a delicious, economical, and nutritious supper.

BROWN (BEEF) STOCK

1 lb. cracked marrow bones
2 lbs. beef shin, cut into 1-inch cubes
1 quart water
½ cup diced onions
¼ cup diced carrots

¼ cup diced celery
1 sprig parsley, minced
¼ teaspoon thyme
¼ teaspoon marjoram
8 peppercorns
5 cloves
1 tablespoon salt

Heat pressure cooker. Melt marrow; brown beef cubes. Stir in remaining ingredients. Close cover securely. Place pressure regulator on vent pipe. COOK 15 MINUTES. Let pressure drop of its own accord. Strain. 4 servings.

Beef stock is used as the basis for many soups and sauces. A clear broth or bouillon makes an appealing appetizer!

Every Italian family has its own version of this wonderful whole-meal soup.

MINESTRONE

1½ lbs. beef bones
1 quart water
3 tablespoons cooking oil
1 clove garlic
1 tablespoon salt
⅛ teaspoon pepper
. . . . .
1 onion, chopped
¼ cup chopped green pepper
½ cup diced celery

1 cup peas
1 cup string beans
1½ cups shredded cabbage
⅔ cup corn
1 cup diced carrots
3 tomatoes, peeled and quartered
. . . . .
1½ cups cooked elbow macaroni
¼ cup grated cheese

Combine beef bones, water, oil, garlic, salt, and pepper in pressure cooker. Close cover securely. Place pressure regulator on vent pipe. COOK 15 MINUTES. Let pressure drop of its own accord. Strain broth. Stir in remaining ingredients, except macaroni and cheese. Close cover securely. Place pressure regulator on vent pipe. COOK 3 MINUTES. Let pressure drop of its own accord. Ladle soup over macaroni in individual soup bowls. Garnish with grated cheese. 4 to 6 servings.

A sophisticated version of the popular hamburger-vegetable soup using red wine in the broth.

TUREEN OF VEGETABLES

2 tablespoons butter
1 onion, chopped
1 lb. ground beef
1 clove garlic, minced
1 cup sliced carrots
1 cup sliced celery
1 cup cut green beans
1 4-ounce can mushrooms
½ cup rice

4 cups stewed tomatoes
1 cup red cooking wine
1 cup water
1 tablespoon minced parsley
½ teaspoon basil
¼ teaspoon thyme
1 bay leaf
½ teaspoon salt
⅛ teaspoon pepper

Heat pressure cooker. Melt butter; brown onion, ground beef, and garlic. Add remaining ingredients and mix. Close cover securely. Place pressure regulator on vent pipe. COOK 15 MINUTES. Let pressure drop of its own accord. 4 to 6 servings.

MENU IDEA
Tureen of Vegetables
Pineapple and Cantaloupe Rings
interlocked, with honey dressing
Homemade Bread and Butter
Butterscotch Pecan Sundaes

BEER BOUILLON WITH CABBAGE

1½ lbs. cabbage, coarsely shredded
2 cups chicken bouillon

1 cup beer
½ teaspoon pepper

Combine ingredients in pressure cooker. Close cover securely. Place pressure regulator on vent pipe. COOK 5 MINUTES. Cool pressure cooker at once. Garnish with grated cheese, if desired. 4 to 6 servings.

POPEYE'S PORK BALL SOUP

1½ lbs. ground pork	¼ teaspoon pepper
1 small onion, grated	2 eggs, beaten
1 teaspoon garlic salt	6 cups chicken
1 teaspoon soy sauce	consomme
½ teaspoon ground ginger	1 10-ounce package
2 tablespoons cornstarch	frozen chopped spinach

Combine ground pork, onion, garlic salt, soy sauce,
ginger, cornstarch, pepper, and eggs. Mix well and
shape into meat balls. Heat pressure cooker. Brown
meat balls. Add consomme. Close cover securely.
Place pressure regulator on vent pipe. COOK 15 MINUTES.
Let pressure drop of its own accord. Add spinach and
cook 3 minutes in open pressure cooker. 4 to 6 servings.

Variation: Substitute 1½ lbs. ground turkey for pork.
Brown turkey balls in a small amount of shortening.

Hint: If some soup is left, freeze and reheat another
day adding cooked thin noodles and more consomme.

Sour cream lends a continental touch.

MEATY TOMATO SOUP

1 lb. short ribs	1 clove garlic
3 cups water	1 teaspoon lemon juice
1 large onion, chopped	½ teaspoon salt
2 carrots, sliced	⅛ teaspoon pepper
1½ cups shredded cabbage	1 teaspoon sugar
2¼ lbs. tomatoes, peeled and quartered	1 cup sour cream
	2 tablespoons cornstarch
1 bay leaf	Hot cooked rice

Combine all ingredients except sour cream, cornstarch and rice in pressure cooker. Close cover securely. Place pressure regulator on vent pipe. COOK 20 MINUTES. Let pressure drop of its own accord. Mix sour cream and cornstarch together until smooth. Gradually stir in 1 cup of soup. Pour mixture into remaining soup, stirring constantly. Heat soup. Place rice in soup bowls before filling with hot soup. 4 to 6 servings.

Like Grandma used to make.

BEEF SOUP, NEW ORLEANS STYLE

1 lb. soup meat, diced	2 cloves garlic, minced
1 small soup bone	2 cups stewed tomatoes
3 cups water	1 cup cooked corn
1 large onion, chopped	1 cup chopped okra
3 large tomatoes, peeled and chopped	¼ cup rice
	⅛ teaspoon cayenne
½ green pepper, chopped	Salt and pepper

Place soup meat, soup bone, water, onion, tomatoes, green pepper, garlic, and stewed tomatoes in pressure cooker. Close cover securely. Place pressure regulator on vent pipe. COOK 20 MINUTES. Let pressure drop of its own accord. Remove soup bone. Add remaining ingredients. Close cover securely. Place pressure regulator on vent pipe. COOK 0 MINUTES. Let pressure drop of its own accord. 4 to 6 servings.

Note: Fresh tomatoes provide attractive chunks, canned tomatoes provide juice.

Join the trend to try South American cuisine.

LATIN AMERICAN ONION SOUP

¼ cup olive oil
4 red onions, sliced
2 green peppers, cut into thin strips
1 teaspoon garlic salt
6 cups beef stock
1 tomato, peeled and chopped
1 cup diced ham
⅛ teaspoon pepper
¼ teaspoon nutmeg
4 egg yolks
¼ cup sherry

Heat pressure cooker. Add olive oil; sauté onions and green pepper. Add garlic salt, beef stock, tomato, ham, pepper, and nutmeg. Close cover securely. Place pressure regulator on vent pipe. COOK 10 MINUTES. Let pressure drop of its own accord. Beat egg yolks until light and stir in sherry. Slowly add a little of the hot soup to mixture, beating constantly. Gradually stir into soup. Garnish with a little nutmeg. 4 to 6 servings.

SOUTH-OF-THE-BORDER SUPPER
Latin American Onion Soup
Corn Bread or Corn Chips
Greens with Oil-and-Vinegar Dressing
Caramel Custard Pudding
Coconut Cupcakes or Cookies

"HOT" RICE SOUP

3 tablespoons olive oil
1 cup rice
2 onions, chopped
1 green pepper, chopped
2 cloves garlic, minced
1 tablespoon minced parsley
2 quarts chicken broth
4 tomatoes, peeled and chopped
½ teaspoon dried ground chili peppers
⅛ teaspoon oregano
⅛ teaspoon basil
Salt

Heat pressure cooker. Add olive oil; sauté rice, onions, green pepper, garlic, and parsley. Add remaining ingredients and stir. Close cover securely. Place pressure regulator on vent pipe. COOK 5 MINUTES. Let pressure drop of its own accord. 4 to 6 servings.

Using white wine as part of the soup stock takes this soup out of the ordinary.

LAMB SOUP WITH CORN MEAL DUMPLINGS

1½ lbs. lamb stew meat, cut into strips
¼ cup flour
2 tablespoons cooking oil
4 cups water
2 cups dry white wine
10 small white onions
2 teaspoons salt
1 teaspoon basil
¼ teaspoon pepper
2 cups diced celery

4 cups diced carrots

. . . . .

½ cup yellow corn meal
½ cup sifted all-purpose flour
2 teaspoons baking powder
½ teaspoon salt
½ cup milk
2 tablespoons salad oil

Dredge lamb with flour. Heat pressure cooker. Add oil; brown lamb. Add water, wine, onions, salt, basil, pepper, celery, and carrots. Close cover securely. Place pressure regulator on vent pipe. COOK 10 MINUTES. Let pressure drop of it own accord.

Sift corn meal, flour, baking powder, and salt. Combine milk and salad oil; add to dry ingredients. Stir just until moistened. Drop from tablespoons on bubbling stew. Remove sealing ring from cover. Place cover loosely on pressure cooker, without pressure regulator. STEAM 15 MINUTES. 4 to 6 servings.

SUPPER SUGGESTION
Fresh Fruit Cup
Lamb Soup with Corn Meal Dumplings
Assorted Relishes
Chocolate-Vanilla Parfaits

Good, whether wrapped in a bun and buried with relish or added to a steaming chowder.

KRAUT 'N FRANK CHOWDER

¼ cup butter or margarine
1 lb. wieners, cut into
  ½-inch chunks
2 large onions, chopped
1 stalk celery, chopped
1 16-ounce can
  sauerkraut, drained

1 bay leaf
¼ teaspoon pepper
¼ teaspoon thyme
1 tablespoon instant beef
  bouillon
3 cups water

Heat pressure cooker. Add butter; brown wieners. Remove wieners. Sauté onion and celery until tender. Stir in wieners, sauerkraut, bay leaf, pepper, thyme, bouillon, and water. Close cover securely. Place pressure regulator on vent pipe. COOK 5 MINUTES. Let pressure drop of its own accord. 4 to 6 servings.

LET DAD AND THE KIDS FIX SUPPER
Kraut 'N Frank Chowder
Garlic-buttered French Bread
Salad of Apple and Grapefruit Slices
Butterscotch Instant Pudding

Smooth, creamy and so good for you.

POTATO 'BAGA SOUP

1 lb. rutabaga, diced
1 lb. potatoes, diced
1 teaspoon salt
1 cup water

3 cups milk
1 teaspoon sugar
2 tablespoons butter

Place rutabaga, potato, salt, and water in pressure cooker. Close cover securely. Place pressure regulator on vent pipe. COOK 5 MINUTES. Cool pressure cooker at once. Mash vegetables. Add remaining ingredients and heat through. Serve hot. If desired, garnish with croutons and paprika. 4 to 6 servings.

*This delicious soup for which,
according to the Bible,
Abraham's older son sold his
birthright to his brother, Jacob.
So thick it's almost stew.*

ESAU'S POTTAGE

½ cup dried lentils	1½ cups stewed tomatoes
1 tablespoon salad oil	½ cup diced celery
1 teaspoon salt	½ cup sliced carrots
Water	½ cup diced parsnips
· · · · ·	½ cup diced green pepper
¼ cup salad oil	1 teaspoon salt
2 onions, sliced	½ teaspoon pepper
1 lb. ground lamb	2 cups water

Soak lentils overnight in oil, salt, and enough water to cover completely. Drain and discard liquid.

Heat pressure cooker. Add oil; sauté onions. Brown ground lamb. Stir in lentils and remaining ingredients. Close cover securely. Place pressure regulator on vent pipe. COOK 20 MINUTES. Let pressure drop of its own accord. 4 to 6 servings.

Variation: Substitute 1 lb. ground beef for the ground lamb.

*A hearty soup chock-full of
meat and vegetables.*

CURRIED LAMB TOMATO SOUP

2 lbs. lamb soup bone	½ cup diced carrots
4 tomatoes, peeled and quartered	¼ cup chopped parsley
	½ teaspoon salt
¼ cup diced green pepper	½ teaspoon curry powder
1 cup chopped celery	1 bay leaf, crumbled
1 cup chopped onion	4 cups water

Combine all ingredients in pressure cooker. Close cover securely. Place pressure regulator on vent pipe. COOK 10 MINUTES. Let pressure drop of its own accord. 4 to 6 servings.

*A must in November, delicious
all year around.*

PILGRIM SOUP

3 lbs. turkey, cut into
serving pieces
6 cups chicken broth
1 onion, chopped
4 carrots, sliced
2 stalks celery, sliced
1 bay leaf

¼ teaspoon poultry
seasoning
¼ teaspoon pepper
1 10-ounce package
frozen corn
2 tablespoons minced
parsley

Place turkey, broth, onion, carrots, celery, bay leaf,
poultry seasoning, and pepper in pressure cooker.
Close cover securely. Place pressure regulator on
vent pipe. COOK 15 MINUTES. Let pressure drop of its
own accord. Remove turkey and set aside. Discard bay
leaf. Strain soup, pressing vegetables through strainer.
Pour soup into pressure cooker. Cut turkey into bite-sized
pieces, discarding skin and bones. Add turkey, corn, and
parsley to soup. Simmer in open pressure cooker until
corn is tender. 4 to 6 servings.

*The holiday turkey is good to
the last drop ... of soup.*

TURKEY VEGETABLE SOUP

2 cups diced turkey
½ cup chopped celery
1 large onion, sliced
½ cup chopped carrots
1 cup canned tomatoes
¼ cup chopped parsley

½ bay leaf
1 teaspoon salt
¼ teaspoon pepper
⅛ teaspoon mace
4 cups water

Combine all ingredients in pressure cooker. Close cover
securely. Place pressure regulator on vent pipe.
COOK 5 MINUTES. Let pressure drop of its own accord.
4 to 6 servings.

Chicken Cacciatore (page 88)

←

19

FISH CHOWDER, SOUTHERN STYLE

2 tablespoons olive oil

2 onions, cut into
¼-inch slices

2 potatoes, cut into
⅓-inch pieces

6 tomatoes, peeled and
chopped

4 cloves garlic, minced

½ teaspoon dried basil

1 bay leaf

½ teaspoon salt

⅛ teaspoon pepper

1 cup water

2 6½-ounce cans minced
clams

1 lb. fillet of sole, cut
into 1-inch pieces

¾ cup okra, cut into
1-inch chunks

Place olive oil, onions, potatoes, tomatoes, garlic, basil, bay leaf, salt, pepper, water, and clam liquid into pressure cooker. Close cover securely. Place pressure regulator on vent pipe. COOK 3 MINUTES. Cool pressure cooker at once. Stir in clams, sole and okra. Simmer until sole is firm, about 5 minutes. 4 to 6 servings.

Elegant . . . excellent

SUCCULENT SHRIMP BOWL

¼ cup butter
1½ lbs. shrimp,
   shelled and cleaned
½ cup chopped
   mushrooms
1 small onion, sliced
3 cups chicken broth

1 cup white cooking wine
1 bay leaf
⅛ teaspoon marjoram
1 stalk celery
½ teaspoon salt
⅛ teaspoon pepper
⅛ teaspoon mace

Heat pressure cooker. Melt butter; sauté shrimp, mushrooms, and onion. Stir in remaining ingredients. Close cover securely. Place pressure regulator on vent pipe. COOK 5 MINUTES. Let pressure drop of its own accord. Thicken soup, if desired. 4 to 6 servings.

This soup hails from San Francisco and is now justly famous throughout the country. Pronounced "chio-pina" the name means chopped soup.

QUICK CRAB CIOPPINO

3 tablespoons olive oil
   or cooking oil
1 onion, chopped
1 stalk celery, sliced
1 tablespoon minced
   parsley
1 clove garlic, crushed
1 green pepper, cut into
   strips
2 cups stewed tomatoes
1 8-ounce can tomato sauce

⅛ teaspoon thyme
⅛ teaspoon rosemary
⅛ teaspoon oregano
1½ teaspoons salt
¼ teaspoon pepper
½ cup dry white wine
1 12-ounce package
   frozen spilt crab legs
1 lb. halibut, cut into
   1½-inch cubes

Heat pressure cooker. Add olive oil, onion; sauté celery, parsley, and garlic. Stir in remaining ingredients. Close cover securely. Place pressure regulator on vent pipe. COOK 2 MINUTES. Cool pressure cooker at once. Serve Cioppino in soup bowls with crusty French bread, if desired. 4 to 6 servings.

MANHATTAN CLAM CHOWDER

5 slices bacon, diced
1 cup sliced onion
3 cups cubed potatoes
1 stalk celery
½ bay leaf
1 teaspoon dried thyme
2 teaspoons salt
¼ teaspoon black pepper

½ green pepper, minced
3½ cups whole canned tomatoes
2 carrots, diced
4 cups water
2 8-ounce cans clams
1 tablespoon diced fresh parsley

Brown bacon in pressure cooker. Sauté onion.
Add potatoes, celery, bay leaf, thyme, salt, pepper,
green pepper, tomatoes, carrots, two cups water, and
clam liquid. Close cover securely. Place pressure
regulator on vent pipe. COOK 5 MINUTES. Let pressure
drop of its own accord. Add remaining two cups water,
clams and parsley. SIMMER 5 MINUTES in open
pressure cooker. 4 to 6 servings.

*THE CHOWDER CONTROVERSY: New England says it is
chowder's birthplace. So does New York. New Englanders call
Manhattan chowder 'vegetable soup with a clam drawn through
it.' New Yorkers say New England chowder is a stew fit
for infants and invalids. Those with unprejudiced palates
will want to sample both before taking sides.*

NEW ENGLAND CLAM CHOWDER

4 slices bacon, chopped
2 cups chopped onions
4 cups cubed potatoes
2 teaspoons salt
⅛ teaspoon pepper

2 cups water
2 8-ounce cans minced clams
1 quart light cream
¼ cup butter

Sauté bacon and onions in pressure cooker. Add
potatoes, salt, pepper, and water. Close cover securely.
Place pressure regulator on vent pipe. COOK 5 MINUTES.
Let pressure drop of its own accord. Drain clams.
Slowly add clams, 1 cup clam liquid, cream and
butter. Stir constantly. SIMMER 10 MINUTES in open
pressure cooker. 4 to 6 servings.

Plan a New Orleans supper when you serve Gumbo: French bread slathered with butter and wedges of pecan pie for dessert.

CRAB GUMBO

2 tablespoons butter
1 large onion, chopped
1 green pepper, chopped
6 tomatoes, peeled and quartered
2 tablespoons chopped parsley
1 bay leaf
1 clove garlic, minced

¼ teaspoon thyme
⅛ teaspoon cayenne
1 tablespoon salt
2 cups chicken broth
2 cups water
¼ cup rice
1½ lbs. crab meat
3 cups okra, cut into ½-inch pieces

Heat pressure cooker. Melt butter; sauté onion and green pepper. Add tomatoes, parsley, bay leaf, garlic, thyme, cayenne, salt, chicken broth, water, and rice. Close cover securely. Place pressure regulator on vent pipe. COOK 3 MINUTES. Cool pressure cooker at once. Add crab meat and okra. SIMMER 5 MINUTES in open pressure cooker. 4 to 6 servings.

Variation: To make Chicken Gumbo, use 1½ to 2 lbs. cut-up frying chicken in place of crab meat.

*Called Christmas Eve Chowder
in many Scandinavian homes,
when it is served with fruited
holiday breads and fruit soup
for dessert.*

CODFISH CHOWDER

1 lb. codfish fillets, cut
  into chunks
2 cups diced potatoes
½ cup chopped celery
½ cup chopped onion
2 tablespoons chopped
  pimiento

1½ teaspoons salt
½ cup water
1 tablespoon flour
2 cups milk
3 slices bacon, cooked
  and crumbled

Place codfish, potatoes, celery, onion, pimiento, salt,
and water in pressure cooker. Close cover securely.
Place pressure regulator on vent pipe. COOK 7 MINUTES.
Cool pressure cooker at once. Blend flour into milk and
stir into chowder. Simmer, stirring until slightly thickened.
Garnish chowder with bacon. 4 to 6 servings.

*One of the best-kept secrets
of good cooking is the way
chicken broth and milk or
cream combine for rich flavor.*

PERCH BISQUE

1 lb. perch fillets, cut
  into bite-sized pieces
¼ cup chopped onion
¼ cup diced carrots
¼ cup diced celery
½ teaspoon salt
¼ teaspoon paprika

1 cup chicken broth
. . . . .
¼ cup flour
3 cups milk
2 ounces cheddar cheese,
  cubed

Place perch, onion, carrot, celery, salt, paprika, and
chicken broth in pressure cooker. Close cover securely.
Place pressure regulator on vent pipe. COOK 7 MINUTES.
Cool pressure cooker at once. Blend flour into milk
and add to pressure cooker. Simmer, stirring until
slightly thickened. Stir in cheese. 4 to 6 servings.

Hint: If you have a blender, this soup may be creamed
until smooth just before serving.

Plan a party around this very special soup. Set out soup, hot bread, salad, and beverage at different spots in dining area, living room and/or kitchen. Guests circulate and serve themselves.

SHRIMP AND CRAB KETTLE

1 green pepper, diced
1 red pepper, diced
2 carrots, sliced
6 tomatoes, peeled and quartered
1 onion, chopped
3 cups chicken broth
1½ cups chopped celery
1 teaspoon salt
¼ teaspoon turmeric
4 whole cloves
½ teaspoon basil

⅛ teaspoon thyme
1 bay leaf
¼ teaspoon crushed dried hot red pepper
. . . . .
1 lb. shrimp, peeled and cleaned
½ lb. crab meat
¼ cup lemon juice
1 tablespoon chopped parsley

Combine green pepper, red pepper, carrots, tomatoes, onion, chicken broth, celery, salt, and turmeric in pressure cooker. Make a bouquet garni of cloves, basil, thyme, bay leaf, and red pepper. Place in pressure cooker. Close cover securely. Place pressure regulator on vent pipe. COOK 5 MINUTES. Cool pressure cooker at once.

Remove bouquet garni. Add remaining ingredients. Close cover securely. Place pressure regulator on vent pipe. COOK 2 MINUTES. Cool pressure cooker at once. 4 to 6 servings.

For an old-country supper, serve this soup with dark Russian rye bread and for dessert fresh fruit to eat "in hand."

BLACK BEAN SOUP

1 cup dried black beans	4 cups vegetable broth
2 tablespoons cooking oil	¼ teaspoon pepper
½ tablespoon salt	¼ teaspoon cayenne
Water	¼ teaspoon dry mustard
. . . . .	2 tablespoons lemon juice
½ cup chopped onion	1 lemon, sliced
1 cup chopped celery	1 hard-cooked egg, sliced
2 tablespoons butter	lengthwise

Wash dried beans and soak overnight in oil, salt, and enough water to cover completely. Drain and discard liquid.

Place beans in pressure cooker. Add remaining ingredients except lemon and egg. Close cover securely. Place pressure regulator on vent pipe. COOK 35 MINUTES. Let pressure drop of its own accord. Garnish each serving with slices of lemon and egg. 4 to 6 servings.

This nutritious soup should be a mainstay in every soup-cook's repertoire.

VEGETARIAN PEA SOUP

1 cup dried whole green
   or yellow peas
2 tablespoons cooking oil
1½ teaspoons salt
   Water
  . . . . .
5 vegetable bouillon
   cubes
⅛ teaspoon black pepper

1 teaspoon salt
1 bay leaf, crumbled
2 tablespoons chopped
   green pepper
2 tablespoons chopped
   carrots
½ cup diced celery
1 onion, chopped
6 cups water

Soak peas overnight in oil, salt, and enough water to cover completely. Drain and discard liquid.

Place peas and remaining ingredients in pressure cooker. Close cover securely. Place pressure regulator on vent pipe. COOK 5 MINUTES. Let pressure drop of its own accord. 4 to 6 servings.

Variation: To make Pea Soup with Ham, add 1 cup cut-up leftover ham to Vegetarian Pea Soup.

GOURMET MEALS

Properly this chapter should be titled, Meals for Gourmets, that is, those with discriminating tastes, those appreciative of the unusual, the continental in cuisine.

Here we have attempted to exploit the versatility of the pressure cooker by using it to produce two, three, even four foods for a festive meal.

As the famed gourmet-teacher James Beard has said, "It is not the basic cost of the food but the care with which it is selected and prepared that makes it gourmet rather than pedestrian."

These are meals for which you will want to do some advance planning — get out your prettiest tablecloth, those cherished goblets, china and silver, even splurge on fresh flowers. Candlelight, by all means, and wine, if the budget allows.

As with any food which you hope will impress those to whom you serve it, prepare the foods for the family in advance so that, on the big day, you will be confident about the meal and enjoy the occasion yourself.

ISLAND ADVENTURE
Polynesian Pork
Celery 'n Mushrooms Island Style
Sesame Seed Crescent Rolls
Macadamia Fruit Basket
Green Tea

POLYNESIAN PORK

1 tablespoon shortening
4 lbs. center cut pork loin
½ teaspoon salt
¼ teaspoon seasoned pepper
⅛ teaspoon ground ginger
½ cup water
¼ cup pineapple juice
1 onion, thinly sliced
6 firm yams, pared
½ cup sherry
6 slices pineapple
1 lime, thinly sliced

Heat pressure cooker. Add shortening; brown pork on all sides. Place pork on cooking rack in pressure cooker. Add salt, pepper, ginger, water, pineapple juice, onion, and yams. Do not fill pressure cooker over ⅔ full. Close cover securely. Place pressure regulator on vent pipe. COOK 50 MINUTES. Let pressure drop of its own accord. Place roast and yams on a heated platter; keep warm. Stir sherry, pineapple and 3 lime slices into sauce in pressure cooker. Bring to a boil; COOK 2 MINUTES. Discard cooked lime slices. Garnish roast with pineapple and fresh lime slices. Glaze pork roast with a ladle of sauce. Pass remaining sauce. 8 servings.

*Use a sharp knife to slice the
mushrooms into little "T" shapes.*

CELERY 'N MUSHROOMS ISLAND STYLE

3 cups diced celery	**3 tablespoons soy sauce**
½ lb. mushrooms, sliced	**2 tablespoons sherry**
¼ teaspoon salt	**1 teaspoon sugar**

Combine all ingredients in pressure cooker. Close cover
securely. Place pressure regulator on vent pipe.
COOK 2 MINUTES. Cool pressure cooker at once.
8 servings.

*If fresh papayas and mangos
are difficult to obtain, look
for a canned tropical fruit
mixture and add the dates to it.*

MACADAMIA FRUIT BASKET

Papaya	**Macadamia nuts, unsalted**
Pineapple	**Brown sugar**
Mangos	**½ cup water**
Dates	

Cut aluminum foil into 6-inch squares. Prepare and
cut fruit into bite-size pieces. Combine fruits and
Macadamia nuts. Place in center of aluminum foil.
Sprinkle brown sugar over fruit. Pinch corners of
aluminum foil together. Place water, cooking
rack, and baskets in pressure cooker. Close cover
securely. Place pressure regulator on vent pipe.
COOK 1 MINUTE. Cool pressure cooker at once.

DINE IN MADRID
Chicken Paella
Ensalada de Escarole
Sopapillas
Bizcocho con Grenadina Sauce (page 208)
Madeira Wine

CHICKEN PAELLA

3 lbs. chicken, cut into serving pieces
2 tablespoons flour
3 tablespoons cooking oil
1 onion, chopped
1 clove garlic, minced
½ teaspoon salt
¼ teaspoon pepper
⅛ teaspoon marjoram

1 cup, bottled or canned, clam juice
1 cup rice
1 green pepper, chopped
4 tomatoes, peeled and quartered
2 7½-ounce cans minced clams
½ lb. shrimp, shelled and deveined

Coat chicken with flour. Heat pressure cooker. Add oil; brown chicken. Sauté onion and garlic. Add salt, pepper, marjoram and clam juice. Close cover securely. Place pressure regulator on vent pipe. COOK 8 MINUTES. Cool pressure cooker at once. Add remaining ingredients. Close cover securely. Place pressure regulator on vent pipe. COOK 0 MINUTES. Let pressure drop of its own accord. 4 to 6 servings.

Ensalada de Escarole

Toss chopped endive or escarole with this dressing: In a mortar, pound 1 clove garlic, 1 tomato, ½ teaspoon pepper, and ½ teaspoon cumin; combine with 3 tablespoons oil and 1½ tablespoons vinegar.

STEAK DINNER ELEGANTE
Filbert-Stuffed Artichokes
Steak à la Bourguinonne
Riz Pilaf à la Valencienne
Popovers
Creme Brulé

Serve this unusual French
vegetable as a festive
first course.

FILBERT-STUFFED ARTICHOKES

½ cup chopped toasted
   filberts
½ cup seasoned dry
   bread crumbs
¼ cup chopped pimiento-
   stuffed olives

1 clove garlic, pressed
2 tablespoons butter,
   melted
4 artichokes, washed
   and trimmed
½ cup water

Combine first five ingredients. Spoon between leaves
of artichokes. Place water, cooking rack, and
artichokes in pressure cooker. Close cover securely.
Place pressure regulator on vent pipe. COOK 10
MINUTES. Cool pressure cooker at once. Serve with
melted butter, if desired. 4 servings.

STEAK À LA BOURGUINONNE

2 slices bacon, diced
2 lbs. round steak, cut
  into serving pieces
1 4-ounce can mushrooms,
  drained

12 small onions
½ cup red wine

Cook bacon in pressure cooker. Brown meat. Add
mushrooms, onions, and wine. Close cover securely.
Place pressure regulator on vent pipe. COOK 15
MINUTES. Cool pressure cooker at once. Thicken
gravy, if desired. 4 servings.

RIZ PILAF À LA VALENCIENNE

½ cup butter
1 cup diced eggplant
1 zucchini squash, diced
2 large mushrooms, sliced
1 clove garlic, minced
1 tomato, peeled and
  chopped

1 7-ounce can pimiento,
  minced
1 teaspoon salt
¼ teaspoon pepper
1 cup rice
2 cups chicken broth

Heat pressure cooker. Add butter; sauté eggplant,
squash, mushrooms, garlic, tomato, and pimiento. Add
salt, pepper, rice, and broth. Close cover securely.
Place pressure regulator on vent pipe. COOK 0 MINUTES.
Let pressure drop of its own accord. If desired,
garnish rice with cooked mussels in their shells.
4 servings.

A GLIMPSE OF POLYNESIA
Malay Duck
Copra Kana
Molokai Carrots
Sherried Dessert Pears
Black Tea

MALAY DUCK

2 teaspoons ground ginger	1 tablespoon shortening
½ teaspoon saffron	1½ cups chopped onions
1½ teaspoons salt	3 cloves garlic, minced
¼ cup soy sauce	¼ teaspoon cayenne
3 lbs. duck, cut into serving pieces	1 cup water
	2 bay leaves

Combine ginger, saffron, salt, and soy sauce; rub mixture into duck. Let stand at room temperature for 1 hour. Heat pressure cooker. Add shortening; brown duck. Remove duck and pour off excess fat. Sauté onion and garlic. Add cayenne and water. Return duck to pressure cooker. Add bay leaves. Close cover securely. Place pressure regulator on vent pipe. COOK 15 MINUTES. Let pressure drop of its own accord. Remove bay leaves. Crisp duck under broiler. Thicken gravy, if desired. 4 servings.

Named for one of the Hawaiian Islands, home of the pineapple.

MOLOKAI CARROTS

2 lbs. carrots, sliced	½ cup pineapple juice
½ teaspoon salt	1 13-ounce can pineapple chunks, drained
2 tablespoons butter	

Place carrots, salt, butter, and pineapple juice in pressure cooker. Close cover securely. Place pressure regulator on vent pipe. COOK 3 MINUTES. Cool pressure cooker at once. Add pineapple chunks and heat through. 4 to 6 servings.

COPRA KANA

½ cup dried grated
  coconut
2 cups water
2 tablespoons butter

¼ cup minced onion
½ teaspoon curry powder
1 cup rice
1 teaspoon salt

Wash coconut under running water to remove sweetness.
Combine coconut and water; bring to a boil. Remove
from heat; let stand 30 minutes.

Press all the liquid from the coconut. Save the
liquid and discard the pulp. Heat pressure cooker.
Add butter; sauté onions. Stir in curry powder, rice,
salt, and coconut liquid. Close cover securely. Place
pressure regulator on vent pipe. COOK 0 MINUTES.
Let pressure drop of its own accord. Stir with a fork;
let stand 5 minutes. 4 servings.

*In summer, use golden
Bartlett pears; in winter,
use D'anjou or Bosc pears.*

SHERRIED DESSERT PEARS

2 tablespoons chopped
  pecans
2 tablespoons raisins
1 tablespoon lemon juice
3 fresh pears, halved
  and cored

¼ cup sherry
¼ cup sugar
¼ cup water

Mix pecans, raisins, and lemon juice. Fill cavity of
each pear half with a small amount of this mixture.
Place pears in pressure cooker. Combine sherry, sugar,
and water. Pour over pears. Close cover securely.
Place pressure regulator on vent pipe. COOK 0 MINUTES.
Cool pressure cooker at once. Garnish with dab of
sour cream or whipped cream cheese. 4 to 6 servings.

DINNER IN GRANADA
Beef Espagnole
Spanish Rice
Espinacas Rellenos Red Peppers
Bread Sticks
Barcelona Chocolate
Cordova Wine

BEEF ESPAGNOLE

3 lbs. rolled beef roast
1 small onion
½ green pepper
1 canned pimiento
1 clove garlic, minced
1 teaspoon salt
¼ teaspoon oregano
¼ teaspoon seasoned pepper

. . . . .
2 tablespoons olive oil
1 8-ounce can tomato sauce
2 tablespoons wine vinegar
1 cup hot water
1 cup stuffed green olives, sliced

Untie roast and spread flat. Chop vegetables, add seasonings and mix well. Spread meat with stuffing, pressing it in well. Re-roll roast; tie firmly.
Heat pressure cooker. Add oil; brown roast well on all sides. Add remaining ingredients. Close cover securely. Place pressure regulator on vent pipe.
COOK 40 MINUTES. Let pressure drop of its own accord. Thicken sauce, if desired. 4 to 6 servings.

SPANISH RICE

1 tablespoon cooking oil
1 large onion, chopped
1 cup diced celery
½ cup diced green pepper

½ teaspoon salt
1 cup rice
2 cups tomato juice

Heat pressure cooker. Add oil; sauté onion, celery, and green pepper. Add remaining ingredients and stir. Close cover securely. Place pressure regulator on vent pipe. COOK 0 MINUTES. Let pressure drop of its own accord. Stir gently with a fork. Garnish rice with crumbled cooked bacon, if desired. 4 servings.

ESPINACAS RELLENOS RED PEPPERS

4 red peppers
1 lb. spinach, chopped
½ teaspoon garlic salt

2 slices cooked bacon,
  crumbled
1 cup water

Cut a one-inch piece from the stem end of the peppers
and scoop out the seeds and fibers. Combine spinach,
garlic salt, and bacon. Stuff the peppers and top
with the stem end. Place water, cooking rack, and
peppers in pressure cooker. Close cover securely.
Place pressure regulator on vent pipe. COOK 5 MINUTES.
Cool pressure cooker at once. 4 servings.

Variation: Green peppers may be used if red ones are
out of season, but eye appeal is not as great.

*Unique . . . a rich dark chocolate
sauce is prepared in the cooker,
then folded into whipped cream.*

BARCELONA CHOCOLATE

¾ cup chopped walnuts
¾ cup sugar
3 ounces chocolate, melted
4 eggs, beaten
⅛ teaspoon salt

1 teaspoon vanilla
2 teaspoons dried lemon
  peel
1 cup water
½ pint whipping cream

Thoroughly combine above ingredients, except water
and whipping cream. Pour into a bowl which will fit
loosely in pressure cooker. Cover with aluminum foil.
Place water, cooking rack, and bowl in pressure cooker.
Close cover securely. Place pressure regulator on
vent pipe. COOK 10 MINUTES. Cool pressure cooker
at once. Whip the cream and fold into pudding. Chill.
4 to 6 servings.

DINNER IN MARSEILLES
Bouillabaisse
Hot French Rolls
Flan
Demitasse

BOUILLABAISSE

3 tablespoons olive oil
2 onions, chopped
4 tomatoes, chopped
1 clove garlic, minced
2 sprigs parsley, chopped
1 bay leaf
1 teaspoon thyme
¼ teaspoon saffron, crushed

4 cups water
1 lb. lobster tail meat, cut into chunks
1 lb. sole fillet, cut into chunks
12 ounces scallops
6 clams in shells, washed

Heat pressure cooker. Add oil; sauté onion. Add next seven ingredients. Close cover securely. Place pressure regulator on vent pipe. COOK 5 MINUTES. Cool pressure cooker at once. Strain the stock and discard the vegetables and herbs. Add the seafood. Close cover securely. Place pressure regulator on vent pipe. COOK 3 MINUTES. Cool pressure cooker at once. Place one clam in each bowl, add soup. 6 servings.

FLAN

⅔ cup sugar
3 eggs, beaten
2 cups light cream

½ teaspoon vanilla
¼ teaspoon almond extract
½ cup water

Heat ⅓ cup sugar over medium heat, stirring constantly, until syrup turns an amber color. Place 1 teaspoon syrup in each of six custard cups. Stir ⅓ cup sugar gradually into beaten eggs. Mix in remaining ingredients, except water. Pour into custard cups. Cover with aluminum foil. Place water, cooking rack, and custard cups in pressure cooker. Close cover securely. Place pressure regulator on vent pipe. COOK 5 MINUTES. Cool pressure cooker at once. Cool flan. Loosen edges with a spatula. Unmold on dessert dishes. 6 servings.

FROM THE RHINELAND
Three-Day Sauerbraten
Potato Dumplings
Sweet-Sour Cabbage
Caraway Rye Bread
Dark Draft Beer
Pfeffernuesse
Black Coffee

Keep the sauerbraten warm in a 200-degree oven, or on an electrified tray, while preparing the cabbage.

SWEET-SOUR CABBAGE

4 slices bacon, diced
1 lb. red cabbage, shredded
1 onion, sliced
¼ cup white raisins

1 teaspoon salt
⅛ teaspoon pepper
2 tablespoons sugar
¼ cup vinegar
¼ cup water

Heat pressure cooker. Brown bacon. Pour off excess drippings. Add remaining ingredients. Close cover securely. Place pressure regulator on vent pipe. COOK 3 MINUTES. Cool pressure cooker at once. Thicken sauce, if desired. 4 to 6 servings.

Sauerbraten is traditional German fare — hearty and flavorful. After marinating and cooking, the meat will nearly fall apart with tenderness.

THREE-DAY SAUERBRATEN

3½ lbs. chuck roast, beef or venison
2 cups vinegar
2 cups water
1 tablespoon salt
½ teaspoon pepper
3 tablespoons brown sugar

3 onions, sliced
1 clove garlic, halved
8 whole cloves
3 bay leaves
5 celery tops

. . . . .

2 tablespoons shortening
12 gingersnaps, crumbled

Place roast in a large earthenware or glass bowl. Heat vinegar and water. Stir in salt, pepper, and brown sugar until dissolved. Top meat with onion slices and pour vinegar around meat. Add remaining ingredients, except shortening and gingersnaps. Cover and refrigerate for three days, turning meat daily.

Remove meat and drain well. Strain liquid and set aside. Heat pressure cooker. Add shortening; brown meat. Add 1 cup of the marinade liquid. Close cover securely. Place pressure regulator on vent pipe. COOK 35 MINUTES. Let pressure drop of its own accord. Place meat on a heated platter. Dilute liquid to strength desired. Add gingersnaps, heat and stir until gravy is smooth. 4 to 6 servings.

Note: The recipe for a milder sauerbraten — marinated only one day — appears on page 49.

MEATS

"*Meat makes the meal,*" *we all agree. Besides being the most costly food in the day's main meal, meat becomes the focal point of an appealing menu. Vegetables must complement it, salads enhance it.*

What cuts of meat to buy and how to cook them is a constant concern and challenge for today's cook. As prices for the tender popular steaks and chops moved well past the dollar-per-pound level, homemakers began turning to the less tender, lower cost, but equally nutritious cuts like beef chuck. And for the pressure cooker, the long cooking required for less-tender cuts is reduced by two-thirds, making it possible to prepare a substantial meal after returning home from a day of work.

Whether you go French with Beef À La Mode, German with Sauerbraten, or American with Corn-Stuffed Pork Chops, let this complete collection of beef, pork, lamb, veal, and variety meats make many a memorable meal.

MEATS — FRESH, FROZEN OR THAWED

The recipes in this chapter were written for fresh or completely thawed meats. If you wish to use frozen meat, thaw it for half an hour or more, just enough so that the meat can be well browned. Then increase the cooking time as given in the recipes: frozen beef and veal should be cooked 25 minutes per pound; frozen pork should cook 30 minutes per pound.

Beef à la Mode was born in the eighteenth century when the extravagant, elaborate Baroque age was at its height. Then, the making of the dish was complicated; now it is streamlined by the use of the pressure cooker.

BEEF À LA MODE

1 cup dry red wine
1 beef bouillon cube
1 cup boiling water
2 onions, chopped
2 cloves garlic, chopped
2 whole cloves
½ teaspoon celery seed
½ teaspoon oregano
½ teaspoon whole peppercorns

2 teaspoons salt
4 lbs. beef pot roast
2 tablespoons shortening
2 tablespoons cornstarch
½ cup water
1 4-ounce can mushroom pieces, drained (optional)

Combine wine, bouillon cube dissolved in boiling water, onions, garlic, and spices in a large bowl. Add meat; cover. Refrigerate overnight, turning meat occasionally.

Remove meat from marinade; drain. Heat pressure cooker. Add shortening; brown meat well on all sides. Add marinade. Close cover securely. Place pressure regulator on vent pipe. COOK 40 MINUTES. Let pressure drop of its own accord. Remove meat from pressure cooker. Combine cornstarch with water; add to liquid in pressure cooker. Heat, stirring constantly until gravy has thickened. Add mushrooms. 8 to 10 servings.

Using beer as a cooking liquid is an age-old idea. Even cooks who do not like beer as a beverage will discover that it increases tenderness and lends a subtle tang that is not at all "beery."

BELGIAN BEEF ROAST

3 lbs. beef roast
2 tablespoons shortening
1 3-ounce can mushrooms with liquid
½ teaspoon salt
⅛ teaspoon pepper

1 onion, chopped
2 tablespoons prepared mustard
2 tablespoons caraway seeds
1 cup beer

Heat pressure cooker. Add shortening; brown roast well on all sides. Combine remaining ingredients; pour over roast. Close cover securely. Place pressure regulator on vent pipe. COOK 30 MINUTES. Let pressure drop of its own accord. Thicken gravy, if desired. 6 to 8 servings.

BEEF IN BEER SAUCE

3 lbs. beef pot roast, cut into 1-inch cubes
1 tablespoon cooking oil
2 cups chopped onion
1 cup beer
½ tablespoon vinegar

2 teaspoons salt
½ teaspoon pepper
1 teaspoon sugar
1 bay leaf
½ teaspoon thyme

Heat pressure cooker. Add oil; brown beef cubes and onion. Add remaining ingredients. Close cover securely. Place pressure regulator on vent pipe. COOK 20 MINUTES. Let pressure drop of its own accord. Serve with potato dumplings, if desired. 6 to 8 servings.

The saltiness of soy sauce and
the sweetness of honey are
matched as in the Far East.

BEEF POT ROAST ORIENTAL

1 teaspoon garlic salt	2 tablespoons soy sauce
½ teaspoon dry mustard	3 tablespoons honey
¼ teaspoon pepper	1 tablespoon vinegar
3 lbs. beef pot roast	1½ teaspoons celery seed
2 tablespoons shortening	½ teaspoon ginger
¾ cup water	

Combine garlic salt, mustard, and pepper; rub into roast.
Heat pressure cooker. Add shortening; brown roast
well on all sides. Combine water, soy sauce, honey,
vinegar, celery seed, and ginger; pour over meat.
Close cover securely. Place pressure regulator on
vent pipe. COOK 40 MINUTES. Let pressure drop of
its own accord. Thicken gravy, if desired. 6 to 8 servings.

All you need to complete
this dinner is fried rice
(page 194), and a salad of
greens and bean sprouts.

PEKING ROAST

4 lb. chuck roast or brisket	1 cup vinegar
3 to 4 cloves garlic, cut into slivers	2 tablespoons shortening
½ small onion, cut into slivers	1 tablespoon instant coffee
	1 cup boiling water
	Salt and pepper

Cut slits in roast. Insert slivers of garlic and onion. Pour
vinegar over roast. Marinate for 24 hours in refrigerator.
Discard vinegar. Heat pressure cooker. Add shortening;
brown roast well on all sides. Dissolve instant coffee in
boiling water; pour over roast. Add salt and pepper.
Close cover securely. Place pressure regulator on
vent pipe. COOK 35 MINUTES. Let pressure drop of
its own accord. If desired, thicken gravy. 8 servings.

Have you been hesitant about serving
Sauerbraten? Try this mild version.

SAUERBRATEN

2 cups water
1 cup wine vinegar
6 peppercorns
2 whole cloves
2 bay leaves

2 onions, chopped
2 teaspoons salt
3 lbs. rolled beef roast
2 tablespoons shortening
1 cup water

Combine 2 cups water, wine vinegar, peppercorns, cloves, bay leaves, onions, and salt. Bring to a boil. Pour over roast; marinate 24 hours in refrigerator.

Drain. Heat pressure cooker. Add shortening; brown roast well on all sides. Add water. Close cover securely. Place pressure regulator on vent pipe. COOK 30 MINUTES. Let pressure drop of its own accord. 6 to 8 servings.

Note: A gourmet meal featuring another version of sauerbraten appears on page 43.

ITALIAN BEEF

4 lbs. rump roast
5 to 6 cloves garlic,
cut into slivers
Salt and pepper
1 cup Marsala wine

2 tablespoons olive oil
1 tablespoon instant coffee
1 cup boiling water
2 3-ounce cans mushrooms
broiled in butter

Cut slits in meat; insert slivers of garlic. Sprinkle salt and pepper over roast. Add wine; marinate 24 hours in refrigerator. Discard wine.
Heat pressure cooker. Add oil; brown roast well on all sides. Dissolve instant coffee in boiling water; pour over meat. Close cover securely. Place pressure regulator on vent pipe. COOK 35 MINUTES. Let pressure drop of its own accord. Thicken gravy, if desired. Add mushrooms; heat through. If desired, garnish with sliced stuffed green olives. 8 to 10 servings.

Many Americans, unaccustomed to the flavor of pure
olive oil, prefer to use a blended oil that is 80%
vegetable oil and 20% olive oil.

This would be the perfect meat around which to plan a cooperative dinner party. You serve the meat, vegetables, and potato or bread. One couple brings a big salad, another a generous dessert. It's a fun way to entertain.

BEEF MANHATTAN

4 lbs. chuck roast
1 tablespoon cooking oil
1 cup red cooking wine
1 clove garlic, crushed
1 green pepper, sliced
1 onion, sliced

1 bay leaf
1 teaspoon parsley
¼ cup catsup
¼ teaspoon salt
⅛ teaspoon pepper

Heat pressure cooker. Add oil; brown roast well on all sides. Combine remaining ingredients; pour over roast. Close cover securely. Place pressure regulator on vent pipe. COOK 35 MINUTES. Let pressure drop of its own accord. If desired, thicken gravy. 8 to 10 servings.

A dressed-up version of braised short ribs. These ribs are apt to be quite fat. Look for the leanest you can find. Allow about 1 pound per person because short ribs are mostly bone.

SHORT RIBS IN RED WINE

3 lbs. short ribs
1 cup red wine
½ onion, diced
1 bay leaf
2 parsley sprigs
¼ teaspoon thyme

1 tablespoon olive oil
¼ teaspoon salt
⅛ teaspoon pepper
1 clove garlic, crushed
2 tablespoons cooking oil
¼ cup water

Cut ribs into serving pieces; place in shallow dish. Combine wine, onion, bay leaf, parsley, thyme, oil, salt, pepper, and garlic; pour over ribs. Cover; chill for several hours or overnight.

Remove ribs; pat dry. Heat pressure cooker. Add oil; brown ribs on all sides. Add marinade and water. Close cover securely. Place pressure regulator on vent pipe. COOK 25 MINUTES. Let pressure drop of its own accord. If desired, thicken gravy. 3 servings.

STEAK IN SAVORY SAUCE

1½ lbs. round steak
2 tablespoons flour
1 tablespoon cooking oil
1 onion, sliced
½ bay leaf
¼ teaspoon rosemary, crushed

1 whole clove
½ teaspoon salt
¼ teaspoon pepper
1 teaspoon parsley flakes
¾ cup beer

Pound flour into steak. Cut meat into serving pieces. Heat pressure cooker. Add oil; brown meat. Add remaining ingredients. Close cover securely. Place pressure regulator on vent pipe. COOK 15 MINUTES. Let pressure drop of its own accord. Thicken gravy, if desired. 4 to 6 servings.

51

The fruit of the lemon, rind and all, adds a distinctive tang to foods, as well as having a tenderizing effect on meats.

LEMONY BEEF

3 lbs. round steak, cut into ½ x 2-inch strips
2 tablespoons shortening Paprika
1 onion, sliced
1 clove garlic, minced
½ teaspoon salt
½ lemon, sliced thin
3 tomatoes, peeled and quartered
1 cup beef broth

Heat pressure cooker. Add shortening; brown meat. Sprinkle paprika over meat while browning. Sauté onion and garlic. Add remaining ingredients. Close cover securely. Place pressure regulator on vent pipe. COOK 5 MINUTES. Cool pressure cooker at once. 6 to 8 servings.

Men will like this dish which calls for "smothering" the steak in cream sauce.

GOURMET STYLE SWISS STEAK

2 lbs. round steak, cut into serving pieces
1 clove garlic
¼ cup flour
2 tablespoons paprika
1 teaspoon salt
¼ teaspoon pepper
3 tablespoons cooking oil
¼ cup sliced onion
1 3-ounce can mushrooms, drained
½ cup water
½ cup sour cream

Rub both sides of meat with cut garlic clove. Combine flour, paprika, salt, and pepper; pound into steak. Heat pressure cooker. Add oil; brown meat. Add onions, mushrooms, and water. Close cover securely. Place pressure regulator on vent pipe. COOK 15 MINUTES. Let pressure drop of its own accord. Place steak on platter. Add sour cream to liquid in pressure cooker; heat through. Thicken sauce, if desired. 4 to 6 servings.

QUICK BEEF ROLL-UPS

1½ cups herb seasoned
    bread stuffing
1 tablespoon prepared
    yellow mustard
½ cup hot water
2 tablespoons butter
6 cube beef steaks

2 tablespoons shortening
1 1½-ounce envelope
    seasoning mix for
    Sloppy Joes
1 6-ounce can tomato
    paste
1½ cups water

Mix bread stuffing, yellow mustard, water, and butter.
Spread a portion of this mixture over each cube beef
steak. Roll steak over stuffing; fasten with skewers or
toothpicks. Heat pressure cooker. Add shortening;
brown steak roll-ups. Combine seasoning mix, tomato
paste, and water. Pour over steak roll-ups. Close cover
securely. Place pressure regulator on vent pipe. COOK 5
MINUTES. Let pressure drop of its own accord.
6 servings.

WELL-BALANCED MEAL
Quick Beef Roll-ups or
Folded Cube Steaks
Baby Lima Beans
Onions in Cream
Fruit Cocktail
Spice Cookies

FOLDED CUBE STEAKS

4 cube beef steaks
¼ teaspoon salt
    Pepper
½ cup bread crumbs
⅛ teaspoon poultry
    seasoning

½ teaspoon minced onion
1 tablespoon water
1 tablespoon cooking oil
¾ cup tomato juice

Sprinkle steaks with salt and pepper. Combine crumbs,
poultry seasoning, onion, and water; cover
each steak with ¼ of mixture. Fold steaks
over stuffing; fasten with skewers or toothpicks.
Heat pressure cooker. Add oil; sear steaks. Add
tomato juice. Close cover securely. Place pressure
regulator on vent pipe. COOK 5 MINUTES. Let pressure
drop of its own accord. 4 servings.

BEEF ROULADES

1½ lbs. round steak
½ cup chopped onion
1 clove garlic, crushed
¼ cup butter
½ cup chopped celery
1 cup herb seasoned bread stuffing
½ cup golden raisins
½ teaspoon salt
¼ teaspoon pepper
2 tablespoons shortening

3 carrots, pared and cut into 1-inch pieces
3 small white onions, peeled
1 cup beef bouillon
2 bay leaves
1 teaspoon dried thyme leaves
½ teaspoon salt
¼ teaspoon black pepper

Pound steak to ¼-inch thick. Cut into 6 x 2-inch pieces. Combine onion, garlic, butter, celery, bread stuffing, raisins, ½ teaspoon salt, and ¼ teaspoon pepper; sauté lightly. Mound stuffing at end of each piece of steak and roll up; tie with string. Heat pressure cooker. Add shortening; brown meat rolls. Add remaining ingredients. Close cover securely. Place pressure regulator on vent pipe. COOK 15 MINUTES. Let pressure drop of its own accord. Thicken gravy, if desired. 4 to 6 servings.

ROULADEN

3 lbs. round steak, ½-inch thick
6 teaspoons prepared mustard
6 slices pressed ham
3 dill pickles, halved lengthwise

2 tablespoons cooking oil
½ cup chopped onions
½ cup chopped celery
1 teaspoon instant beef bouillon
1 cup tomato juice
1 cup sour cream

Cut round steak into 6 pieces. Spread each piece with mustard; top with ham. Place a pickle half at end and roll up; tie with cord. Heat pressure cooker. Add oil; brown meat rolls. Add onions, celery, bouillon, and tomato juice. Close cover securely. Place pressure regulator on vent pipe. COOK 15 MINUTES. Cool pressure cooker at once. Blend sour cream into sauce for gravy. 6 servings.

Whether you call it stuffing or dressing, men love it with moist, tender meat. This is a stuffing turned sophisticate with the addition of nuts and fruit.

TANGERINE PECAN STEAK ROLL

4 tablespoons butter
½ cup chopped onion
½ cup chopped celery
½ cup chopped pecans
2 cups melba toast crumbs
2 teaspoons salt
¼ teaspoon black pepper
½ teaspoon crushed rosemary
1 tablespoon parsley

1 cup chicken broth
1 egg, beaten
2 tangerines, sectioned and snipped into small pieces
3 lbs. round steak, 1-inch thick
Salt and pepper
2 tablespoons shortening
½ cup water

Melt butter in pressure cooker. Sauté onion, celery, and pecans. Remove pressure cooker from heat; add melba toast crumbs, salt, pepper, rosemary, and parsley. Mix in ¼ cup chicken broth, egg, and tangerines. Sprinkle meat with salt and pepper. Spread with stuffing mixture and roll up; tie with cord. Heat pressure cooker. Add shortening; brown meat. Pour remaining chicken broth and water over meat. Close cover securely. Place pressure regulator on vent pipe. COOK 20 MINUTES. Let pressure drop of its own accord. Garnish platter with fluted mushrooms, if desired. 6 to 8 servings.

V.I.P. DINNER
Hot Tomato Bouillon
Tangerine Pecan Steak Roll
Parsley Potatoes
Lettuce-Spinach Salad
Angel Food Cake with Cocoa Whipped Cream

Flank steak is filled with a savory stuffing.

MEDITERRANEAN FLANK STEAK

1 lb. flank steak	1 teaspoon salt
1 tablespoon olive oil	¼ teaspoon marjoram
¼ lb. pork sausage, browned	¼ teaspoon thyme
	⅛ teaspoon pepper
2 onions, chopped	½ cup red wine
1 clove garlic, grated	2 tomatoes, peeled and quartered
½ cup bread crumbs	

Cut steak crosswise into two equal pieces. Heat pressure cooker. Add oil; brown steak. Combine pork sausage, onion, garlic, bread, salt, marjoram, thyme, and pepper. Spread stuffing mixture on one steak; top with remaining steak. Secure with toothpicks. Place steak in pressure cooker. Add wine and tomatoes. Close cover securely. Place pressure regulator on vent pipe. COOK 15 MINUTES. Let pressure drop of its own accord. 4 servings.

SUPPER ROMANA
Mediterranean Flank Steak
Macaroni with Pepper and Pimiento
Italian Green Beans
Citrus Salad   Bread Sticks
Spumoni Ice Cream

BEEF FLANK JARDINIERE

1½ lbs. flank steak	1 teaspoon salt
1 cup grated carrot	1 tablespoon cooking oil
¼ cup grated onion	2 cups canned tomatoes
½ teaspoon celery seed	½ cup beef stock

Score steak to cut fibers. Combine carrots, onion, celery seed, and salt; spread over steak. Roll up; secure with toothpicks or skewers. Heat pressure cooker. Add oil; brown steak. Add tomatoes and beef stock. Close cover securely. Place pressure regulator on vent pipe. COOK 15 MINUTES. Let pressure drop of its own accord. 4 to 6 servings.

SWEET-SOUR BEEF

1½ lbs. round steak,
cut into serving pieces
1 tablespoon cooking oil
¼ cup chopped onion
1 green pepper, cut into
strips
½ teaspoon salt

⅛ teaspoon pepper
⅓ cup soy sauce
3 tablespoons brown sugar
1 teaspoon ground ginger
1 20-ounce can
sliced pineapple

Heat pressure cooker. Add oil; brown steak. Add onion,
green pepper, salt, pepper, soy sauce, brown sugar,
ginger, and pineapple liquid. Close cover securely.
Place pressure regulator on vent pipe. COOK 15
MINUTES. Cool pressure cooker at once. Add pineapple
slices. Close cover securely. Place pressure regulator
on vent pipe. COOK 0 MINUTES. Let pressure drop
of its own accord. Serve with rice, if desired.
4 to 6 servings.

BEEF BOMBAY

4 tablespoons cooking oil
1 cup diced onion
2 lbs. round steak, cut
into ½-inch strips
2 teaspoons salt

1 tablespoon curry powder
1 cup beer
½ cup chopped apple
¼ cup grated coconut
¼ cup slivered almonds

Heat pressure cooker. Add oil; brown onion. Remove
onion; brown round steak. Add onion, salt, curry
powder, and beer. Close cover securely. Place pressure
regulator on vent pipe. COOK 15 MINUTES. Cool
pressure cooker at once. Add apple, coconut, and
almonds. Close cover securely. Place pressure
regulator on vent pipe. COOK 0 MINUTES. Let pressure
drop of its own accord. Serve with rice, if desired.
4 to 6 servings.

INTERNATIONAL BUFFET SUPPER
Sweet-Sour Beef or Beef Bombay
Hot White or Brown Rice
French Green Beans with Mushrooms
Italian Salad
Hawaiian Pineapple Cake

GERMAN STEAK SUPREME

3 lbs. round steak, cut
into 2-inch cubes
3 cups beer
1 cup minced onion
1½ teaspoons salt
¼ teaspoon pepper
3 tablespoons cooking oil

6 carrots, cut in half
lengthwise
1 tablespoon flour
2 tablespoons grated
orange rind
2 tablespoons currant jelly
1 tablespoon lemon juice

Place steak in shallow dish. Combine beer, onion, salt,
and pepper; pour over steak. Cover and chill
12 to 24 hours.

Remove steak; pat dry. Heat pressure cooker.
Add shortening; brown steak. Add 2 cups
marinade and carrots. Close cover securely. Place
pressure regulator on vent pipe. COOK 20 MINUTES.
Cool pressure cooker at once. Place steak in serving
dish. Mix flour with a small amount of water; add
to liquid in pressure cooker along with orange rind,
jelly, and lemon juice. Simmer 5 minutes in open
pressure cooker. Pour sauce over steak cubes.
6 to 8 servings.

DINNER ON TIME
German Steak Supreme
Whipped Potatoes
Buttered Broccoli
Baking Powder Biscuits
Orange Ambrosia

FLAVORFUL BEEF SHANKS

3 lbs. beef shanks
1 teaspoon cooking oil
1 onion, chopped
1 cup red cooking wine
½ cup beef bouillon

½ teaspoon thyme
1 teaspoon Worcestershire
sauce
1 3-ounce can mushrooms,
drained

Heat pressure cooker. Add oil; brown shanks. Add
remaining ingredients. Close cover securely. Place
pressure regulator on vent pipe. COOK 25 MINUTES.
Let pressure drop of its own accord. Thicken sauce,
if desired. 2 to 3 servings.

*Another classic from French
cuisine updated for the
pressure cooker.*

RAGOUT DE BOEUF

2 lbs. round steak, cut
   into narrow strips
½ cup flour
½ teaspoon pepper
2 teaspoons paprika
2 teaspoons garlic salt
2 tablespoons cooking oil

1 onion, sliced
½ cup Burgundy wine
1 8-ounce can button
   mushrooms, drained
½ cup mushroom liquid
   or water

Dredge round steak in a mixture of flour, pepper,
paprika, and garlic salt. Heat pressure cooker. Add
oil; brown steak and onions. Add remaining ingredients.
Close cover securely. Place pressure regulator on
vent pipe. COOK 15 MINUTES. Let pressure drop of
its own accord. Thicken gravy, if desired, and serve
on a bed of hot rice. 4 to 6 servings.

*A sausage forms the surprise
center of this unusual
combination of meats. Excellent
with poppy seed noodles.*

SURPRISE BEEF BOATS

1 lb. ground beef
¼ cup deviled ham
1 cup bread crumbs
½ cup evaporated milk
2 eggs, beaten
10 pork sausages

1 tablespoon salad oil
1 cup brown sugar
½ cup water
½ cup vinegar
1 teaspoon mustard

Combine ground beef, deviled ham, bread crumbs, milk,
and eggs. Divide mixture into 10 equal portions;
wrap around pork sausages. Heat pressure cooker. Add
oil; brown meat. Combine brown sugar, water, vinegar,
and mustard; pour over meat. Close cover securely.
Place pressure regulator on vent pipe. COOK 15 MINUTES.
Cool pressure cooker at once. 4 to 5 servings.

Veal is extremely popular in Italy, France and Austria. But we Americans need recipes like these and suggestions for seasonings to give it flavor.

TENDEREST VEAL ROAST

3 lbs. breast of veal, rolled and tied
2 tablespoons cooking oil
1 cup beer
¾ cup chopped onion

1 bay leaf
Dash of nutmeg
2 teaspoons salt
¼ teaspoon pepper

Heat pressure cooker. Add oil; brown veal on all sides. Combine remaining ingredients; pour over veal. Close cover securely. Place pressure regulator on vent pipe. COOK 50 MINUTES. Let pressure drop of its own accord. Thicken gravy, if desired. 8 to 10 servings.

Veal browns very slowly so take your time because the browning will heighten the flavor. One cook we know reads a favorite magazine while browning meats.

VEAL ROAST CARAWAY

3 lbs. veal roast
2 tablespoons cooking oil
½ cup chopped onion
1 teaspoon salt
2 tablespoons vinegar

2 teaspoons caraway seeds
1 teaspoon paprika
1 teaspoon marjoram
1 cup water

Heat pressure cooker. Add oil; brown roast. Add remaining ingredients. Close cover securely. Place pressure regulator on vent pipe. COOK 45 MINUTES. Let pressure drop of its own accord. Thicken gravy and serve with hot buttered noodles, if desired. 6 to 8 servings.

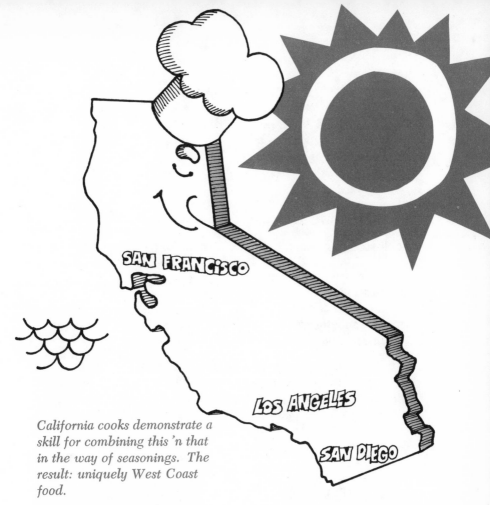

California cooks demonstrate a skill for combining this 'n that in the way of seasonings. The result: uniquely West Coast food.

CALIFORNIA SPECIAL

Flour
Salt and pepper
Paprika
2 lbs. veal round
2 tablespoons cooking oil
1 clove garlic, minced
1 onion, sliced

1 4-ounce can mushrooms with liquid
½ cup white wine
1 teaspoon instant chicken bouillon
¼ cup tomato juice
⅛ teaspoon nutmeg
2 tablespoons parsley

Combine flour, salt, pepper, and paprika. Pound flour mixture into veal; cut into thin strips. Heat pressure cooker. Add oil; brown meat. Add remaining ingredients. Close cover securely. Place pressure regulator on vent pipe. COOK 15 MINUTES. Let pressure drop of its own accord. Thicken gravy, if desired. 4 to 6 servings.

Because veal is immature meat it needs to cook in liquid to avoid dryness. And its bland flavor and smooth texture demand the use of tart, stimulating seasonings.

LEMON-LIME VEAL

3 lbs. veal cutlets, cut into ¼-inch strips
½ teaspoon garlic salt
¼ teaspoon pepper
¼ cup flour
¼ cup cooking oil
1 onion, thinly sliced

2 3-ounce cans mushrooms
1 teaspoon parsley flakes
¼ teaspoon oregano
½ teaspoon salt
1 7-ounce bottle lemon-lime carbonated beverage

Dredge veal with mixture of garlic salt, pepper, and flour. Heat pressure cooker. Add oil; brown veal and onions. Stir in mushrooms, parsley flakes, oregano, salt, and carbonated beverage. Close cover securely. Place pressure regulator on vent pipe. COOK 15 MINUTES. Cool pressure cooker at once. 9 to 12 servings.

VEAL SICILIAN

6 veal cutlets, cut into 1-inch strips
Flour
Salt and pepper
4 tablespoons olive oil
1 onion, chopped
3 tomatoes, peeled and quartered

½ cup white wine
1 bay leaf
¼ teaspoon thyme
½ teaspoon chopped parsley
1 6-ounce can mushrooms with liquid
½ cup sliced ripe olives

Dredge veal in flour seasoned with salt and pepper. Heat pressure cooker. Add olive oil; brown meat. Add all remaining ingredients except mushrooms and olives. Close cover securely. Place pressure regulator on vent pipe. COOK 10 MINUTES. Let pressure drop of its own accord. Add mushrooms and olives; heat through. Thicken sauce, if desired. 6 servings.

VEAL ROLLS

1¼ lbs. veal cutlets
Salt and pepper
¾ cup cracker crumbs
1 teaspoon parsley flakes
1 teaspoon lemon rind
¼ teaspoon thyme
¼ teaspoon basil

3 tablespoons milk
2 tablespoons melted butter
2 tablespoons cooking oil
1 cup chicken broth
1 tablespoon lemon juice

Season veal with salt and pepper. Combine cracker crumbs, parsley, lemon rind, thyme, basil, milk, and butter. Spread on veal cutlets. Roll up, securing with toothpicks or string. Heat pressure cooker. Add oil; brown veal rolls. Combine chicken broth and lemon juice. Pour over veal rolls. Close cover securely. Place pressure regulator on vent pipe. COOK 10 MINUTES. Let pressure drop of its own accord. Thicken gravy, if desired. 3 to 4 servings.

PARISIAN FARE
French Onion Soup
Veal Rolls
Whole Baby Carrots
Green Beans Vinaigrette
French Bread
Folded Crepes with Orange Sauce

VEAL SAUTERNE

2 lbs. veal round,
½-inch thick

3 tablespoons cooking oil

½ cup consomme

½ cup sauterne wine

1 4-ounce can mushrooms
with liquid

1 clove garlic, chopped

2 tablespoons parsley

Salt and pepper

Cut veal into serving pieces. Heat pressure cooker. Add oil; brown meat. Add remaining ingredients. Close cover securely. Place pressure regulator on vent pipe. COOK 15 MINUTES. Let pressure drop of its own accord. Thicken gravy, if desired. 4 to 6 servings.

IT'S THE VEAL THING
Veal Sauterne
Mashed Potatoes with Gravy
Buttered Beets
Orange Onion Ring Salad
Oatmeal Muffins
Butterscotch Pie

CURRIED VEAL WITH RICE

2 tablespoons flour

1 teaspoon salt

⅛ teaspoon pepper

1½ lbs. veal shoulder, cut
into ½-inch pieces

3 tablespoons cooking oil

1 cup diced celery

½ teaspoon curry powder

½ cup water

. . . . .

½ cup rice

¾ cup water

Combine flour, salt, and pepper. Dredge veal pieces. Heat pressure cooker. Add oil; brown veal. Stir in celery, curry powder, and water. Close cover securely. Place pressure regulator on vent pipe. COOK 15 MINUTES.

Cool pressure cooker at once. Stir in rice and water. Close cover securely. Place pressure regulator on vent pipe. COOK 0 MINUTES. Let pressure drop of its own accord. 4 to 6 servings.

*An unusual cold meat course
for a special occasion. You
will need the cut of veal leg
sold for scallopine.*

VEAL ROLL ITALIAN STYLE

4 **thin veal cutlets**
½ **lb. salami, sliced**
½ **lb. bologna, sliced**
½ **lb. cooked ham, sliced**
⅓ **cup packaged stuffing
   mix, finely crushed**
¼ **teaspoon instant
   minced garlic**

¼ **cup minced parsley**
½ **teaspoon basil**
Salt and pepper
2 **tablespoons olive oil**
1 **cup water**
½ **cup red wine**

Place veal cutlets between pieces of waxed paper;
pound until very thin. Arrange slices on another piece of
waxed paper side by side the long way, overlapping
edges slightly. Pound the overlapping edges well so
that they are pressed together. On the veal, arrange
overlapping rows of salami, bologna, and ham. Combine
crumbs, garlic, parsley, basil, salt, and pepper;
sprinkle evenly over layered meats. Dribble with
olive oil. Roll up carefully, but not too loosely.
Tie roll with soft string at about one inch intervals.
Place water, wine, cooking rack, and veal roll in
pressure cooker. Close cover securely. Place pressure
regulator on vent pipe. COOK 15 MINUTES. Cool
pressure cooker at once. Chill roll; serve in slices on
shredded lettuce with Italian style dressing, if desired.
6 servings.

Variation: For Hot Veal Roll, slice the roll as soon as it
is cooked. Serve with thin noodles tossed with butter
and cheese.

Leg of lamb makes a juicy,
flavorful roast and so does the
rib section. This is the same
meat from which the spectacular
crown roast of lamb is made.
It's tender 'n tasty.

TOUCH-OF-DILL LAMB ROAST

3 lbs. lamb rib roast
2 tablespoons cooking oil
1 onion, chopped
2 tablespoons vinegar

2 teaspoons salt
1 teaspoon dill seed
½ teaspoon pepper
1 cup water

Heat pressure cooker. Add oil; brown roast. Add remaining ingredients. Close cover securely. Place pressure regulator on vent pipe. COOK 35 MINUTES. Let pressure drop of its own accord. 4 to 6 servings.

SPRING SPECIAL
Touch-of-Dill Lamb Roast
Bulgur Wheat Pilaf
Buttered Peas and Carrots
Honey Raisin Cake

LAMB CHOPS WITH GRAPES

6 lamb chops,
   ½-inch thick
2 tablespoons cooking oil
1 onion, chopped
2 cloves garlic, minced
1 teaspoon salt
¼ teaspoon pepper

1 cup chicken broth
1 tablespoon butter
¼ lb. mushrooms, sliced
½ cup seedless grapes,
   cut in half
⅓ cup sour cream

Heat pressure cooker. Add oil; brown lamb chops, onion, and garlic. Add salt, pepper, and chicken broth. Close cover securely. Place pressure regulator on vent pipe. COOK 2 MINUTES. Cool pressure cooker at once. Remove lamb chops. Melt butter in fry pan; saute' mushrooms. Stir in mushrooms, grapes, and sour cream. Simmer, stirring until slightly thickened. Serve sauce over lamb chops on bed of rice, if desired. 4 to 6 servings.

*Floridians, many of whom came
from the North, use plentiful
oranges every meal of the day.
Besides wonderful color and
flavor, oranges furnish the
sunshine vitamin, C.*

LAMB FLORIDIAN

**6 lamb chops, 1-inch thick
2 tablespoons cooking oil
Salt and pepper**

**2 oranges, peeled and
sliced thin
½ cup beer**

Heat pressure cooker. Add oil; brown chops. Sprinkle
with salt and pepper. Add orange slices and beer.
Close cover securely. Place pressure regulator on
vent pipe. COOK 10 MINUTES. Let pressure drop
of its own accord. Thicken gravy, if desired.
4 to 6 servings.

Variation: True Floridians will enjoy substituting
orange juice for the beer.

*Whether you choose loin, rib or
shoulder lamb chops, they are
a delicacy to be savored.
Slash outer edge of fat on
chops diagonally at 1-inch
intervals to prevent curling.*

GLAZED LAMB CHOPS

**6 lamb chops,
 ½-inch thick
1 tablespoon cooking oil
½ teaspoon salt**

**¼ teaspoon pepper
½ cup orange juice
½ cup pineapple juice
¼ teaspoon cinnamon**

Heat pressure cooker. Add oil; brown chops. Season
with salt and pepper. Add remaining ingredients. Close
cover securely. Place pressure regulator on vent pipe.
COOK 2 MINUTES. Cool pressure cooker at once.
Thicken sauce, if desired. 4 to 6 servings.

Pineapple is the symbol of hospitality, so why not serve this attractively glazed roast for an impromptu dinner to say "welcome" to a newcomer or "thank you" to a friend?

PINEAPPLE-GLAZED PORK ROAST

3 lbs. pork loin roast	½ teaspoon cinnamon
1 tablespoon cooking oil	1 teaspoon grated orange peel
Salt and pepper	
6 whole cloves	2 tablespoons cornstarch
1½ cups pineapple juice	1 20-ounce can pineapple spears
½ cup water	
2 tablespoons honey	

Trim excess fat from roast. Heat pressure cooker. Add oil; brown roast. Season roast with salt and pepper; stud with cloves. Combine pineapple juice, water, honey, cinnamon, and orange peel; pour over roast. Close cover securely. Place pressure regulator on vent pipe. COOK 45 MINUTES. Let pressure drop of its own accord. Place roast on platter; keep warm.

Drain pineapple spears. Combine syrup and cornstarch; stir into liquid in pressure cooker. Cook until thickened, stirring constantly. Add pineapple spears and heat through. Garnish roast with pineapple spears and a spoonful of gravy. 4 to 6 servings.

SPICED PORK BUTT

3 lbs. pork butt	1 bay leaf
1 tablespoon shortening	2 tablespoons brown sugar
1 onion	
2 whole cloves	1½ cups beer

Heat pressure cooker. Add shortening; brown meat. Pour off excess drippings. Stud onion with cloves. Add onion, bay leaf, brown sugar, and beer. Close cover securely. Place pressure regulator on vent pipe. COOK 60 MINUTES. Let pressure drop of its own accord. 4 to 6 servings.

PEANUTTY PORK ROAST

1 tablespoon sugar
2 teaspoons garlic salt
3 lbs. pork loin roast
1 tablespoon cooking oil
1½ cups water

2 tablespoons flour
½ cup water
½ cup salted peanuts,
   finely chopped

Combine sugar and garlic salt; rub into surface of roast.
Heat pressure cooker. Add oil; brown roast well on
all sides. Add 1½ cups water. Close cover securely.
Place pressure regulator on vent pipe. COOK 60
MINUTES. Let pressure drop of its own accord. Remove
roast. Blend flour and ½ cup water; gradually stir into
hot liquid in pressure cooker. Add peanuts. Simmer,
stirring until slightly thickened. 4 to 6 servings.

Team pork loin roast with sweet potatoes, tart cole slaw, hot rolls and fruit pie.

PORK ROAST WITH ORANGE GLAZE

3 lbs. pork loin roast
1 tablespoon cooking oil
Salt and pepper
6 whole cloves
1½ cups orange juice
½ cup water

2 tablespoons honey
½ teaspoon cinnamon
1 teaspoon grated orange peel
6 orange slices

Trim excess fat from roast. Heat pressure cooker. Add oil; brown roast. Season roast with salt and pepper; stud with cloves. Combine orange juice, water, honey, cinnamon, and orange peel; pour over roast. Close cover securely. Place pressure regulator on vent pipe.
COOK 60 MINUTES. Let pressure drop of its own accord. Place on platter and garnish with orange slices.
4 to 6 servings.

Fresh ham, the cut of the pork leg not cured, makes a sweet, tender pork roast that is even easier to carve than the pork loin.

CASTILIAN STYLE HAM

3 lbs. fresh ham
1 teaspoon olive oil
1 bay leaf, crushed
1 clove garlic, minced
¼ teaspoon thyme
1 tablespoon chopped parsley

1 tablespoon minced onion
1 tablespoon paprika
1 teaspoon salt
3 tablespoons lemon juice
½ cup white wine
1 cup water

Heat pressure cooker. Add oil; brown ham. Pour off drippings. Combine remaining ingredients; pour over ham. Close cover securely. Place pressure regulator on vent pipe. COOK 60 MINUTES. Let pressure drop of its own accord. 8 to 10 servings.

*Pork is most plentiful from
November to February.
It should be well cooked,
but not dried out.*

PORK SHOULDER WITH ONION-FRUIT SAUCE

2 lbs. rolled boneless
  pork shoulder
1 10½-ounce can
  condensed onion soup

¾ cup apple juice
½ cup chopped mixed
  dried fruit
3 whole cloves

Heat pressure cooker. Brown roast well on all sides.
Remove excess drippings. Add soup, apple juice, fruit,
and cloves. Close cover securely. Place pressure
regulator on vent pipe. COOK 40 MINUTES. Let pressure
drop of its own accord. Serve thickened sauce with
meat and rice, if desired. 4 to 6 servings.

*A wonderful idea for a weekend
dinner — whether you are
having guests or not. Any
leftover meat will make
delicious sandwiches.*

PORK POT ROAST

4 lbs. pork loin roast
1 clove garlic, cut into
  slivers
1 tablespoon shortening
¼ teaspoon salt
¼ teaspoon pepper

2 onions, sliced
2 bay leaves
1 whole clove
1½ cups water
2 tablespoons cornstarch
2 tablespoons soy sauce

Make tiny slits in roast; insert slivers of garlic.
Heat pressure cooker. Add shortening; brown roast.
Add salt, pepper, onions, bay leaves, clove, and water.
Close cover securely. Place pressure regulator on
vent pipe. COOK 60 MINUTES. Let pressure drop of
its own accord. Blend cornstarch with soy sauce and
thicken gravy. 6 to 8 servings.

The work of pushing the stuffing into those little "pockets" will be very much worth it when you discover how much the man of the house enjoys these chops.

CORN-STUFFED PORK CHOPS

4 pork loin chops,
1-inch thick with
pocket in each
1 tablespoon shortening
2 tablespoons butter
½ cup chopped celery
¼ cup chopped onion

2 cups soft bread crumbs
½ cup whole kernel corn
¼ teaspoon salt
¼ teaspoon sage
Pepper
½ cup water

Heat pressure cooker. Add shortening; brown pork chops. Remove chops. Melt butter; sauté celery and onion. Add remaining ingredients, except water; combine thoroughly. Stuff chops with dressing mixture. Place water, cooking rack, and chops in pressure cooker. Close cover securely. Place pressure regulator on vent pipe. COOK 10 MINUTES. Let pressure drop of its own accord. 4 servings.

ORANGE PORK STEAKS

6 pork steaks
2 teaspoons cooking oil
Salt and pepper
¼ teaspoon cinnamon
¼ teaspoon ground
cloves

2 teaspoons grated
orange rind
½ cup orange juice
¼ cup sugar
1½ teaspoons cornstrach
6 orange slices

Heat pressure cooker. Add oil; brown pork steaks. Add salt, pepper, cinnamon, cloves, orange rind, and orange juice. Close cover securely. Place pressure regulator on vent pipe. COOK 15 MINUTES. Cool pressure cooker at once. Remove the steaks. Add sugar and cornstarch. Heat until thickened, stirring constantly. Glaze orange slices in the sauce. Spoon sauce over pork steak; garnish with orange slices. 6 servings.

PORK CHOPS À LA PEACH

6 **pork chops**
1 **tablespoon shortening**
2 **teaspoons lemon juice**
½ **teaspoon cinnamon**
6 **cloves**

½ **teaspoon salt**
⅛ **teaspoon pepper**
3½ **cups canned peach halves**

Heat pressure cooker. Add shortening; brown chops.
Combine lemon juice, cinnamon, cloves, salt, pepper,
and peach syrup. Pour over pork chops. Close cover
securely. Place pressure regulator on vent pipe.
COOK 15 MINUTES. Cool pressure cooker at once.
Place pork chops on a heated platter. Add peach halves;
heat through. Thicken sauce, if desired. 6 servings.

DINNER STARRING CHOPS
Pork Chops à la Peach
Corn on the Cob
Sliced Tomatoes and Cucumbers
Hot Onion Bread
Mint Ice Cream
Chocolate Cookies

*For good smooth gravy, measure liquid in pressure cooker;
pour back into pressure cooker. For each cup of liquid, shake
together ¼ cup cold water and 2 tablespoons flour. Stir flour
mixture slowly into liquid. Heat to boiling, stirring constantly.
Boil 1 minute.*

From Louisiana comes the spicy Creole cuisine now nationally famous. Unique foods, like these chops, were created when French and Spanish dishes were prepared by African cooks using American ingredients.

PORK CHOPS IN SPICY CREOLE SAUCE

6 pork chops
2 tablespoons cooking oil
½ cup minced celery
⅓ cup minced green pepper
¼ cup minced onion
2 tomatoes, peeled and cut into chunks
1 teaspoon salt
⅛ teaspoon pepper
1 clove garlic, minced
1 chicken bouillon cube
1 cup boiling water
¼ cup barbecue sauce
3 tablespoons molasses
2 tablespoons cornstarch
¼ cup water

Heat pressure cooker. Add oil; brown chops. Remove chops. Sauté celery, green pepper, and onion. Add tomatoes, seasonings, bouillon cube dissolved in hot water, barbecue sauce, and molasses; mix well. Replace pork chops. Close cover securely. Place pressure regulator on vent pipe. COOK 10 MINUTES. Let pressure drop of its own accord. Remove chops from pressure cooker. Combine cornstarch with water. Add to liquid in pressure cooker. Heat, stirring constantly until gravy has thickened. Pour over chops. 6 servings.

Variation: Substitute lean pork shoulder, cut into 1-inch cubes, for pork chops.

As more and more Americans ·
have traveled in the Orient or
been in military service there,
our appreciation for and
interest in Oriental cookery
has grown. These chops are
typical in combining meat
and fruit and in the use of
ginger and soy sauce.

PORK CHOPS ORIENTAL

4 rib pork chops,
  1-inch thick
2 tablespoons shortening
2 tablespoons instant
  chopped onion
1 8½-ounce can
  pineapple slices
1 tablespoon prepared
  mustard

1 teaspoon salt
⅛ teaspoon black pepper
⅛ teaspoon ground ginger
½ cup condensed beef
  broth
3 tablespoons cornstarch
1 tablespoon soy sauce

Have butcher butterfly chops. Heat pressure cooker.
Add shortening; brown chops. Stir in onion; brown
lightly. In pressure cooker, arrange alternate layers of
chops and pineapple slices, starting with chops. Combine
mustard, salt, pepper, ginger, broth, and pineapple juice.
Pour over chops. Close cover securely. Place pressure
regulator on vent pipe. COOK 8 MINUTES. Let pressure
drop of its own accord. Place chops and pineapple on
heated platter. Blend cornstarch and soy sauce with a
small amount of water. Stir into sauce. Simmer until
slightly thickened. 4 servings.

Pork steaks are every bit as delicious and nutritious as chops and usually cost less.

COMPANY PORK STEAK

1 tablespoon flour
1 teaspoon thyme
½ teaspoon garlic salt
1 teaspoon paprika
4 pork steaks

1 tablespoon cooking oil
1 onion, sliced
½ cup chicken stock
4 lemon slices
4 green pepper rings

Combine flour, thyme, garlic salt, and paprika; sprinkle over both sides of steak. Heat pressure cooker. Add oil; brown pork steaks. Add onion and chicken stock. Close cover securely. Place pressure regulator on vent pipe. COOK 15 MINUTES. Cool pressure cooker at once. Add lemon and green pepper. Close cover securely. Place pressure regulator on vent pipe. COOK 3 MINUTES. Cool pressure cooker at once. Thicken gravy, if desired. 4 servings.

PORK STEAK WITH HERB GRAVY

6 pork steaks
1 tablespoon shortening
1 onion, chopped
¼ teaspoon salt
½ teaspoon oregano

¼ teaspoon marjoram
2 tablespoons parsley flakes
½ cup water

Heat pressure cooker. Add shortening; brown steaks. Combine onion, salt, oregano, marjoram, and parsley flakes; sprinkle over meat. Add water. Close cover securely. Place pressure regulator on vent pipe. COOK 15 MINUTES. Let pressure drop of its own accord. Thicken gravy, if desired. 6 servings.

Spices, like the oregano and marjoram called for here, can become dry in a warm cupboard. "Awaken" the flavor of each dried herb by rubbing it with the fingers of your right hand while holding it in the palm of your left hand. The warmth, moisture, and natural oils of your hands do the trick!

*This cheesey custard tastes
much like the renowned
Quiche Lorraine — an egg,
ham and cheese pie.*

HAM AND CHEESE CUSTARD

2 slices cooked bacon,
  crumbled
2 eggs, beaten
1½ cups milk
1 teaspoon grated onion
¼ teaspoon salt

3 slices boiled ham, cut
  into 1-inch squares
4 ounces Swiss cheese,
  shredded
½ cup water

In a bowl, combine eggs, milk, onion, and salt. Add
ham and cheese, reserving a small amount of cheese for
topping; mix. Pour into custard cups. Top with bacon
and remaining cheese. Cover with aluminum foil. Place
water, cooking rack, and custard cups in pressure cooker.
Close cover securely. Place pressure regulator on vent
pipe. COOK 5 MINUTES. Cool pressure cooker at once.
4 to 6 servings.

*WEEKEND BRUNCH
Compote of Fruits in Season
Ham and Cheese Custard
Cinnamon Streusel Coffeecake*

HAM HOCKS OR SHANKS

4 lbs. ham hocks or
  shanks
2 tablespoons shortening
1 onion, sliced
1 teaspoon salt

½ teaspoon thyme
¼ teaspoon sage
¼ teaspoon savory
6 peppercorns
1 cup water

Heat pressure cooker. Add shortening; brown ham
hocks. Add remaining ingredients. Close cover securely.
Place pressure regulator on vent pipe. COOK 45
MINUTES. Let pressure drop of its own accord.
4 servings.

Tired of tomatoey barbecue sauces? Try this sweet-spicy one.

SPARERIBS MILWAUKEE STYLE

2½ lbs. spareribs
1 cup beer
⅓ cup honey
2 teaspoons lemon juice
1 teaspoon salt

1½ teaspoons dry mustard
½ teaspoon ground ginger
⅛ teaspoon nutmeg
1 tablespoon cooking oil

Cut spareribs into serving size pieces; place in shallow dish. Combine beer, honey, lemon juice, salt, mustard, ginger, and nutmeg. Pour over ribs. Cover; chill for several hours or overnight. Heat pressure cooker. Add oil; brown ribs. Pour ½ cup marinade in pressure cooker. Close cover securely. Place pressure regulator on vent pipe. COOK 15 MINUTES. Let pressure drop of its own accord. Remove ribs. Thicken gravy, if desired. 2 to 3 servings.

Variation: Substitute 3 lbs. pork roast for the spareribs. COOK 60 MINUTES, in 1½ cups marinade.

SPARERIBS WITH AN ITALIAN ACCENT

3 lbs. spareribs, cut into serving pieces
1 tablespoon olive oil
12 artichoke hearts
2½ cups canned tomatoes

3 cloves garlic, minced
½ teaspoon salt
⅛ teaspoon sage
⅛ teaspoon rosemary

Heat pressure cooker. Add oil; brown spareribs. Place artichokes around meat. Combine remaining ingredients; pour over meat. Close cover securely. Place pressure regulator on vent pipe. COOK 15 MINUTES. Let pressure drop of its own accord. 3 to 4 servings.

When November rolls around and you have mincemeat in the house for fragrant pies, try it with other foods. Then, just for fun, make the family guess what the sweet-tart ingredient is in the ribs' sauce.

HOLIDAY SPARERIBS

2½ lbs. spareribs,
   cut into serving pieces
1 tablespoon shortening

1 cup prepared mincemeat
1 cup beef bouillon
2 tablespoons vinegar

Heat pressure cooker. Add shortening; brown ribs. Combine remaining ingredients; pour over ribs. Close cover securely. Place pressure regulator on vent pipe. COOK 15 MINUTES. Let pressure drop of its own accord. Thicken gravy, if desired. Garnish with colorful red pickled apple slices. 2 to 3 servings.

ORANGE GLAZED RIBS

3 lbs. country style
   spareribs
1 tablespoon cooking oil
½ cup brown sugar
1 teaspoon grated orange
   peel

⅔ cup orange juice
¼ cup soy sauce
½ teaspoon ginger
1 clove garlic, crushed

Trim ribs of excess fat. Heat pressure cooker. Add oil; brown ribs. Combine remaining ingredients; pour over ribs. Close cover securely. Place pressure regulator on vent pipe. COOK 15 MINUTES. Cool pressure cooker at once. 4 to 6 servings.

Liver is an important source of iron in the diet.

BACON, LIVER AND ONIONS

1½ lbs. beef liver, cut
   into serving pieces
   Boiling water
½ cup flour
½ teaspoon salt

⅛ teaspoon pepper
6 slices bacon
1 onion, chopped
½ cup water

Pour boiling water over liver. Let stand 5 minutes. Drain.
Combine flour, salt, and pepper. Dredge liver in seasoned
flour. Fry bacon; remove from pressure cooker.
Pour off excess drippings. Brown liver; remove from
pressure cooker. Sauté onion. Place water, cooking
rack, and liver in pressure cooker. Close cover
securely. Place pressure regulator on vent pipe.
COOK 5 MINUTES. Cool pressure cooker at once.
Thicken gravy, if desired. Garnish with bacon.
4 to 6 servings.

Try it ... you'll like it!

LIVER NAPOLI

1 lb. liver
   Boiling water
3 tablespoons flour
2 slices bacon, chopped
1 onion, chopped
1 clove garlic, minced
1 green pepper, chopped
¼ cup mushrooms

1 20-ounce can whole
   tomatoes
¼ cup water
¼ teaspoon oregano
½ teaspoon celery seed
1 teaspoon salt
⅛ teaspoon pepper

Pour boiling water over liver. Let stand 5 minutes.
Drain. Cut liver into ¼-inch cubes; dredge
in flour. Fry bacon; remove from pressure cooker.
Pour off excess drippings. Brown liver, onion, garlic,
and green pepper. Add remaining ingredients.
Close cover securely. Place pressure regulator on
vent pipe. COOK 5 MINUTES. Cool pressure cooker
at once. Serve on spaghetti and sprinkle with
Parmesan cheese, if desired. 4 servings.

BEEF LIVER ROLLS

1½ lbs. beef liver,
  cut into serving pieces
  Boiling water
 1 cup seasoned stuffing
  croutons
 ¼ cup beef broth
 ½ teaspoon salt
 ⅛ teaspoon pepper
 ¼ cup chopped celery

3 tablespoons butter,
  melted
1 tablespoon chopped
  onion
2 tablespoons flour
1 teaspoon salt
⅛ teaspoon pepper
3 tablespoons bacon
  drippings
½ cup water

Pour boiling water over liver. Let stand 5 minutes.
Drain. Combine croutons, broth, salt, pepper, celery,
butter, and onion. Spread dressing on liver. Roll
lengthwise; fasten with toothpicks. Combine flour,
salt, and pepper. Dip liver rolls in seasoned flour.
Heat pressure cooker. Add bacon drippings; brown
liver rolls. Place water, cooking rack, and liver rolls
in pressure cooker. Close cover securely. Place
pressure regulator on vent pipe. COOK 8 MINUTES.
Cool pressure cooker at once. 4 to 6 servings.

DOUBLE DELIGHT TONGUE

3½ lbs. smoked tongue
  Cold water
 3 cups water
 1 10¾-ounce can
  condensed mushroom
  soup

½ cup sour cream
1 teaspoon horseradish
1 teaspoon lemon juice

Cover tongue with water. Soak 1 to 2 hours; drain.
Place 3 cups water, cooking rack, and tongue in pressure
cooker. Close cover securely. Place pressure regulator
on vent pipe. COOK 55 MINUTES. Let pressure drop of
its own accord. Remove tongue; rinse and skin. Pour
water from pressure cooker and remove cooking rack.
Blend remaining ingredients in pressure cooker. Add
tongue. Place cover loosely on pressure cooker without
pressure regulator. Heat through. Thin sauce with water,
if desired. Serve sauce over tongue. 8 to 10 servings.

POULTRY

"Chicken every Sunday" is a familiar American folkway, and for generations, doting grandmas have doled out a drumstick for every child when chicken was served.

Yes, chicken, together with turkey and game birds, is favorite American fare. No wonder, when you consider its low cost, low calorie count, and low cholesterol level.

These fair means with fowl demonstrate the ease with which chicken lends itself to a wide choice of seasonings, flavorings, sauces, and accompaniments. As you browse through the chapter, you will notice we borrowed — with all due appreciation — chicken specialties from the Chinese, the East Indians, the Russians, and the French.

If you are not already enjoying poultry once a week, for variety and economy, let the ideas in this chapter tempt you to try new ways with chicken, turkey, Cornish game hens, or duck.

If your family prefers the meaty chicken parts to the bony ones, you may want to buy 1 pound each of breasts, legs, and thighs for these recipes.

ORIENTAL CHICKEN WITH WALNUTS

3 lbs. chicken, cut into
  serving pieces
2 tablespoons cooking oil
¼ cup soy sauce
1 teaspoon sugar
1 teaspoon salt

1 cup walnuts, chopped
½ teaspoon ginger
1 cup water
1 8-ounce can bamboo
  shoots
1 tablespoon cornstarch

Heat pressure cooker. Add oil; brown chicken. Add next six ingredients. Close cover securely. Place pressure regulator on vent pipe. COOK 10 MINUTES. Cool pressure cooker at once. Remove chicken to platter. Add bamboo shoots and cornstarch, stirring until slightly thickened. Ladle sauce over chicken. 4 to 6 servings.

For an authentic, exotic garnish for either of these dishes, toast 1 cup sunflower nutmeats in dry skillet over medium heat, stirring constantly. When roasted, sprinkle with Japanese soy sauce and toss to mix well.

BREAST OF CHICKEN TAHITIAN

2 chicken breasts, split
  Paprika
2 tablespoons cooking oil
1 6-ounce can frozen
  pineapple-orange juice
  concentrate

¼ cup butter
1 teaspoon ginger
1 teaspoon soy sauce

Sprinkle chicken breasts with paprika. Heat pressure cooker. Add oil; brown chicken. Combine juice, butter, ginger, and soy sauce; heat until blended. Pour sauce over chicken in pressure cooker. Close cover securely. Place pressure regulator on vent pipe. COOK 10 MINUTES. Cool pressure cooker at once. Thicken gravy, if desired. 4 servings.

CHICKEN ALMONDINE

2½ lbs. chicken, cut
    into serving pieces
Paprika
1 tablespoon cooking oil
Salt and pepper

1 10¼-ounce can cream
    of mushroom soup
½ cup water
¼ cup slivered almonds

Sprinkle chicken with paprika. Heat pressure cooker.
Add oil; brown chicken. Season with salt and pepper.
Combine cream of mushroom soup with water; pour
over chicken. Close cover securely. Place pressure
regulator on vent pipe. COOK 10 MINUTES. Cool
pressure cooker at once. Add almonds to gravy
and thicken, if desired. 4 to 5 servings.

FAMILY FAVORITE
Chicken Almondine
over Toast Points
Peas and Onions
Jellied Fruit Medley
Peppermint Ice Cream

Mild chicken takes kindly to
a trip through the herb
garden — or shelf.

CHICKEN WITH HERB SAUCE

3 lbs. chicken, cut into
    serving pieces
6 tablespoons cooking oil
½ cup white wine
1 clove garlic, peeled
    and grated
1 onion, peeled and grated

½ teaspoon salt
½ teaspoon celery salt
½ teaspoon pepper
¼ teaspoon thyme
¼ teaspoon oregano
¼ teaspoon rosemary

Heat pressure cooker. Add 2 tablespoons oil; brown
chicken. Blend remaining ingredients; pour over
chicken. Close cover securely. Place pressure
regulator on vent pipe. COOK 10 MINUTES. Cool
pressure cooker at once. Thicken gravy, if desired.
4 to 6 servings.

A word to the wise: for smooth sauce, watch and stir carefully so that cream does not boil or it may curdle.

SHERRIED CHICKEN

3 chicken breasts, halved
2 tablespoons cooking oil
2 teaspoons salt

½ cup sherry
1 4-ounce can button mushrooms
1 cup sour cream

Heat pressure cooker. Add oil; brown chicken. Sprinkle with salt. Add sherry, mushrooms, and liquid. Close cover securely. Place pressure regulator on vent pipe. COOK 10 MINUTES. Cool pressure cooker at once. Remove chicken. Add sour cream to hot liquid in pressure cooker. Simmer, stirring until slightly thickened. 6 servings.

FANCY FIXIN'S
Sherried Chicken
Rice-Almond Casserole
Spinach-Lettuce-Radish Bowl
Hot Biscuits
Pears à la mode with Chocolate Sauce

CHICKEN STEW CONTINENTAL

3 lbs. chicken breasts, cut into 2-inch pieces
2 tablespoons olive oil
4 small white onions, peeled
4 whole cloves
½ clove garlic, finely minced

½ cup chopped celery
1 tablespoon parsley
1 teaspoon thyme
2 shallots, chopped
5 tomatoes, peeled and quartered
½ teaspoon saffron
2 cups chicken broth

Heat pressure cooker. Add olive oil; brown chicken. Add remaining ingredients. Close cover securely. Place pressure regulator on vent pipe. COOK 10 MINUTES. Let pressure drop of its own accord. 4 to 6 servings.

A most attractive dish, worthy of a special guest. The orange juice acts as both tenderizer and glamorizer.

CHICKEN IN ORANGE SAUCE

3 lbs. chicken, cut into
   serving pieces
   Paprika
2 tablespoons margarine
2 teaspoons salt
⅛ teaspoon cinnamon
⅛ teaspoon ginger

½ cup white raisins
½ cup slivered almonds
1½ cups orange juice
   Cornstarch
1 cup water
1 fresh orange, peeled
   and sectioned

Sprinkle chicken lightly with paprika. Heat pressure cooker. Add margarine; brown chicken. Season with combined salt, cinnamon, and ginger. Add raisins, almonds, and orange juice. Close cover securely. Place pressure regulator on vent pipe. COOK 10 MINUTES. Cool pressure cooker at once. Remove chicken from pressure cooker. Combine cornstarch with water; add to liquid in pressure cooker. Heat, stirring constantly, until sauce has thickened. Pour sauce over chicken and garnish with orange sections. Serve on white rice, if desired. 4 to 6 servings.

For Perfect Orange Sections: Rather than peeling the orange as you would to eat in hand, use paring knife and peel round and round cutting close to flesh. Then take knife and release fruit section by section. This method eliminates all the white membrane which may impart a bitter taste.

CHICKEN CACCIATORE

3 lbs. chicken, cut
   into serving pieces
   Salt and pepper
3 tablespoons shortening
1 1½-ounce envelope
   spaghetti sauce mix
1 6-ounce can tomato
   paste

1¾ cups water
1 4-ounce can sliced
   mushrooms
1 8-ounce package
   spaghetti, cooked

Sprinkle chicken with salt and pepper. Heat pressure
cooker. Add shortening; brown chicken. Combine
spaghetti sauce mix, tomato paste, and water; pour over
chicken. Add mushrooms with liquid. Close cover
securely. Place pressure regulator on vent pipe.
COOK 10 MINUTES. Cool pressure cooker at once.
Serve chicken over hot cooked spaghetti. 4 to 6 servings.

CHICKEN WITH SPANISH RICE

3 lbs. chicken, cut into
  serving pieces
2 tablespoons cooking oil
2 onions, chopped
2 cloves garlic, minced
1 green pepper, chopped
1 cup tomato juice
1 cup beer

1 teaspoon chicken
  bouillon
2 teaspoons salt
½ teaspoon saffron
1 cup water
1 cup rice
1 10-ounce package
  frozen green peas

Heat pressure cooker. Add oil; brown chicken.
Remove from pressure cooker. Sauté onion, garlic, and
green pepper. Add chicken and next six ingredients.
Close cover securely. Place pressure regulator on
vent pipe. COOK 10 MINUTES. Cool pressure cooker
at once. Remove chicken and keep warm. Add rice and
green peas to pressure cooker. Close cover securely.
Place pressure regulator on vent pipe. COOK 0 MINUTES.
Let pressure drop of its own accord. Serve on
rice mixture. 4 to 6 servings.

Variation: To make Chicken with Risotto, omit green
pepper and saffron. Substitute 1 cup chicken broth and
1 cup white wine for tomato juice and beer.

CHICKEN LIVERS WITH MUSHROOMS

2 slices bacon
2 lbs. chicken livers,
  cut into ½-inch pieces
1 4-ounce can mushrooms,
  drained

1 teaspoon salt
⅛ teaspoon pepper
½ cup water

Fry bacon in pressure cooker; remove. Sauté liver.
Pour off excess drippings. Add remaining ingredients.
Close cover securely. Place pressure regulator on
vent pipe. COOK 5 MINUTES. Cool pressure cooker
at once. Crumble bacon; sprinkle over liver.
6 to 8 servings.

Dress-up treatment for a
nutritious but neglected
part of the chicken.

CHICKEN GIZZARDS

1 lb. chicken gizzards
2 cups chicken broth
2 tablespoons chopped
  parsley
  Cornstarch

½ teaspoon salt
¼ teaspoon pepper
¼ cup Burgundy wine
  Slivered, toasted almonds

Place gizzards, broth, and parsley in pressure cooker.
Close cover securely. Place pressure regulator on
vent pipe. COOK 30 MINUTES. Cool pressure cooker
at once. Remove gizzards from broth; slice thin.
Thicken broth with cornstarch. Add seasonings, sliced
gizzards, and wine. Reheat and serve on toast points,
if desired. Garnish with toasted almonds. 4 servings.

CHICKEN CALCUTTA

3 lbs. chicken, cut
   into serving pieces
2 tablespoons shortening
1 onion, chopped
1 green pepper, diced
2 tomatoes, peeled and
   quartered
2 teaspoons salt

1 teaspoon curry powder
1 teaspoon coriander
1 teaspoon cumin
1 teaspoon turmeric
¼ teaspoon cinnamon
¼ teaspoon garlic powder
½ teaspoon black pepper
½ cup water

Heat pressure cooker. Add shortening; brown chicken.
Add remaining ingredients. Close cover securely.
Place pressure regulator on vent pipe. COOK 10 MINUTES.
Cool pressure cooker at once. Thicken sauce and
serve with brown rice, if desired. 4 to 6 servings.

*In India and Pakistan, cooks compound their own spice
mixtures for seasoning their curries of meat or vegetables.
They may use as many as 12 fresh herbs and spices —
garlic, coriander, and cumin among them.*

INDIAN CHICKEN STEW

3 lbs. stewing chicken,
   cut into serving pieces
2 cups water
2 onions, chopped
1 teaspoon salt
¼ teaspoon pepper
¼ teaspoon cloves

¼ teaspoon ginger
¼ teaspoon cinnamon
¼ teaspoon mace
½ teaspoon saffron
2 tablespoons raisins
½ cup rice

Place chicken in pressure cooker. Combine remaining
ingredients; pour over chicken. Close cover
securely. Place pressure regulator on vent pipe.
COOK 15 MINUTES. Let pressure drop of its own
accord. 6 to 8 servings.

CHICKEN CANTONESE

3 lbs. chicken, cut into serving pieces
2 tablespoons shortening
1 teaspoon salt
¼ teaspoon pepper
½ cup pineapple juice
½ cup orange juice

¼ teaspoon ground cloves
¼ teaspoon nutmeg
2 tablespoons cornstarch
½ cup pineapple tidbits
1 orange, sectioned
½ cup slivered almonds

Heat pressure cooker. Add shortening; brown chicken. Add salt, pepper, pineapple juice, orange juice, cloves, and nutmeg. Close cover securely. Place pressure regulator on vent pipe. COOK 10 MINUTES. Cool pressure cooker at once. Remove chicken. Thicken juices with cornstarch. Add pineapple tidbits, orange sections, and almonds; heat through. Serve on hot rice, if desired. 4 to 6 servings.

Hour in Hawaii — the day you serve either of these chicken dishes, plan a fun dinner hour Hawaiian style. Put on some island music, have the children make paper leis, and serve the meal on a low table with everyone sitting around cross-legged (shoes off, of course).

GINGER PEACHY CHICKEN

3 lbs. chicken, cut into serving pieces
2 tablespoons shortening
2 teaspoons salt
⅛ teaspoon pepper
½ teaspoon ground ginger

2 teaspoons soy sauce
1 29-ounce can peach halves
2 tablespoons cornstarch
¼ cup water

Heat pressure cooker. Add shortening; brown chicken. Combine salt, pepper, ground ginger, soy sauce, and peach syrup. Pour over chicken. Close cover securely. Place pressure regulator on vent pipe. COOK 10 MINUTES. Cool pressure cooker at once. Place chicken on a heated platter. Combine cornstarch and water. Stir into liquid in pressure cooker. Cook until thickened, stirring constantly. Add peach halves; heat through. 4 to 6 servings.

CHICKEN FRICASSEE WITH PARSLEY SAUCE

2 tablespoons cooking oil
1 clove garlic, sliced
3 lbs. chicken, cut into
serving pieces
1½ teaspoons salt
½ cup water
. . . . .
2 tablespoons butter

2 tablespoons flour
1 cup chicken stock
1 cup light cream
½ cup chopped parsley
½ teaspoon salt
2 egg yolks, beaten
1 tablespoon lemon juice

Heat pressure cooker. Add oil; brown garlic. Remove garlic; brown chicken. Season with salt. Add water. Close cover securely. Place pressure regulator on vent pipe. COOK 10 MINUTES. Cool pressure cooker at once.

Melt butter in a saucepan; blend in flour. Add stock, cream, parsley, and salt, stirring constantly. Bring to a boil. Combine egg yolks and lemon juice. Add to sauce; heat, stirring constantly, until sauce has thickened. Ladle sauce over chicken on serving platter. 4 to 6 servings.

CHICKEN CURRY

3 lbs. chicken, cut
into serving pieces
2 tablespoons shortening
2 teaspoons curry powder
2½ teaspoons salt

2 onions, chopped
1 teaspoon vinegar
1 cup water
2 tablespoons cornstarch
¼ cup water

Heat pressure cooker. Add shortening; brown chicken. Season with combined curry powder and salt. Add onions, vinegar, and water. Close cover securely. Place pressure regulator on vent pipe. COOK 10 MINUTES. Cool pressure cooker at once. Place chicken on a heated platter. Combine cornstarch and water. Stir into liquid in pressure cooker. Cook until thickened, stirring constantly. Ladle sauce over chicken. 4 to 6 servings.

Cornish hens — and other whole meats — look appealing on a platter. Surround them with rice on one side, a green vegetable on the other.

YANKEE CORNISH HENS

2 Cornish game hens
½ teaspoon salt
¼ teaspoon pepper
2 teaspoons tarragon leaves, crumbled
2 tablespoons cooking oil
1 onion, diced
½ cup minced green onion

2 carrots, diced
1 cup diced celery
1 tablespoon chopped parsley
1 bay leaf
4 tomatoes, peeled and quartered
½ cup white cooking wine

Season Cornish hens with salt and pepper. Sprinkle 1 teaspoon tarragon in cavity of each hen. Heat pressure cooker. Add oil; brown hens. Remove hens.
Sauté onions, carrots, and celery. Add remaining ingredients. Place hens in pressure cooker. Close cover securely. Place pressure regulator on vent pipe.
COOK 8 MINUTES. Let pressure drop of its own accord. Thicken sauce, if desired. 2 to 4 servings.

It's easy to bone chicken parts.
Using a keenly sharp knife,
slice right to bone of the thigh.
Then gently but firmly pull
meat against blade of knife,
releasing meat from bone.

MINI CHICKEN ROLLS

6 chicken thighs, boned
½ teaspoon salt
¼ cup bread crumbs
2 tablespoons finely
  chopped celery
1 tablespoon finely
  chopped onion
1 tablespoon parsley
2 tablespoons cooking oil
1 cup water

Place boned thighs skin side down. Combine, salt,
bread crumbs, celery, onion, and parsley. Divide among
boned thighs. Fold sides over stuffing, fasten with
toothpicks or small skewers. Heat pressure cooker.
Add oil; brown chicken rolls. Add water. Close cover
securely. Place pressure regulator on vent pipe.
COOK 10 MINUTES. Cool pressure cooker at once.
6 servings.

Variation: For a larger serving, substitute boned chicken
breasts for thighs.

Hint for Dieters: Chicken is excellent for calorie watchers —
if the skin and its accompanying fat are removed.

*This is the perfect entree for a
just-for-two holiday dinner.*

CORNISH HENS IN CURRANT SAUCE

1 cup seasoned stuffing
   croutons
¼ cup wheat germ
¼ cup chopped celery
¼ cup chicken broth
3 tablespoons butter,
   melted
½ teaspoon sugar
1 teaspoon salt

Dash pepper
2 tablespoons cooking oil
2 Cornish game hens
½ cup golden raisins
2 teaspoons lemon juice
¼ teaspoon ground
   allspice
½ cup chicken broth
½ cup red currant jelly

Combine first 8 ingredients; stuff Cornish hens. Heat
pressure cooker. Add oil; brown hens. Add remaining
ingredients except jelly. Close cover securely. Place
pressure regulator on vent pipe. COOK 8 MINUTES.
Cool pressure cooker at once. Remove hens from
pressure cooker. Blend jelly into sauce; heat through.
Brush hens with sauce; crisp under a broiler.
Garnish with crabapples, if desired.
2 to 4 servings.

DUO THANKSGIVING
Broiled Grapefruit
Cornish Hens in Currant Sauce
Acorn Squash Halves
filled with Peas
Whole Wheat Rolls
Mincemeat Tarts

Buy these tiny birds for festive
dinners. They are usually
12 to 16 ounces each.

STUFFED GAME HENS

3 slices bacon, diced
1 onion, chopped
4 chicken livers, chopped
¼ cup raisins
1 cup soft bread crumbs

¼ cup sherry
2 Cornish game hens
Salt and pepper
½ cup water

Fry bacon in pressure cooker. Pour off excess drippings. Sauté onion and liver. Add raisins, bread crumbs, and sherry. Stuff hens; brown in bacon drippings. Remove hens from pressure cooker; sprinkle with salt and pepper. Place water, cooking rack, and hens in pressure cooker. Close cover securely. Place pressure regulator on vent pipe. COOK 8 MINUTES. Let pressure drop of its own accord. Place hens under broiler, if crispness is desired. 2 to 4 servings.

HENS WITH PINEAPPLE WALNUT STUFFING

2 tablespoons butter
¼ cup water
¼ cup packaged
   stuffing mix
1 egg, slightly beaten
¼ cup drained, crushed
   pineapple

2 tablespoons finely
   chopped walnuts
2 Cornish game hens
2 tablespoons cooking oil
½ teaspoon salt
⅛ teaspoon pepper
1 cup water

Heat butter in ¼ cup water until melted. Stir in stuffing mix, egg, pineapple, and walnuts. Stuff hens with mixture. Heat pressure cooker. Add oil; brown hens. Season with salt and pepper. Add water. Close cover securely. Place pressure regulator on vent pipe. COOK 8 MINUTES. Cool pressure cooker at once. Crisp hens under broiler. 2 to 4 servings.

DUCKLING À L'ORANGE

3 lbs. duckling
1 tablespoon cooking oil
2 unpeeled oranges, quartered
1 clove garlic, chopped

1 teaspoon salt
2 whole black peppercorns
½ cup Burgundy wine
½ cup orange marmalade

Heat pressure cooker. Add oil; brown duckling.
Stuff duckling cavity with oranges, garlic, salt, and
peppercorns. Combine Burgundy and marmalade. Pour
over duckling in pressure cooker. Close cover securely.
Place pressure regulator on vent pipe. COOK 15
MINUTES. Let pressure drop of its own accord.
Remove stuffing before serving. Thicken sauce,
if desired. 3 to 4 servings.

DINNER MENU FROM THE WHITE HOUSE
Duckling à L'Orange
Wild Rice
French Green Beans
Chocolate Mousse
Demitasse

*If you are not lucky enough to
have a hunter in the family,
enjoy domestic duck from the
poultry department. The beer
broth aids and abets the duck's
natural dark, rich flavor.*

GAMBRINUS DUCK

3 lbs. duck, disjointed	¾ cup beer
1 tablespoon cooking oil	1 cup chicken stock
2 onions, diced	⅛ teaspoon thyme
3 tablespoons flour	⅛ teaspoon basil

Remove as much fat as possible from the duck. Heat
pressure cooker. Add oil; brown duck. Remove from
pressure cooker. Pour off excess fat; brown onions.
Stir in flour, beer, chicken stock, thyme, and basil.
Replace duck. Close cover securely. Place pressure
regulator on vent pipe. COOK 15 MINUTES. Let
pressure drop of its own accord. Remove duck.
Thicken gravy, if desired. 3 to 4 servings.

WEEKEND DINNER
Gambrinus Duck
White-Brown Rice Casserole
Cauliflower with Bacon Bits
Orange Ambrosia Salad
Cheesecake

This famous Russian dish has become a favorite in this country and there are versions for every conceivable type of meat. Typically served with buttered noodles or fluffy rice.

DUCKLING STROGANOFF

3 lbs. duckling
1 teaspoon salt
1 teaspoon dry mustard
⅛ teaspoon pepper
⅛ teaspoon marjoram
1 tablespoon cooking oil
1 onion, sliced

1 3-ounce can sliced mushrooms
¼ cup water
2 tablespoons sherry
1 tablespoon cornstarch
½ cup sour cream
2 tablespoons catsup

Skin duckling. Remove meat from bones; cut into ½ x 2 inch strips. Toss lightly with combined salt, mustard, pepper, and marjoram. Heat pressure cooker. Add oil; brown duckling. Sauté onion. Add mushrooms and water. Close cover securely. Place pressure regulator on vent pipe. COOK 3 MINUTES. Cool pressure cooker at once. Combine sherry with cornstarch. Add to liquid in pressure cooker. Heat, stirring constantly, until sauce has thickened. Add combined sour cream and catsup. Mix thoroughly; heat through. 3 to 4 servings.

*Poultry and fruit are
natural meal mates.*

PINEAPPLE DUCKLING

1 20-ounce can crushed
  pineapple
1 tablespoon soy sauce
¼ teaspoon ginger
½ teaspoon salt
¼ teaspoon pepper
4 lbs. duckling, cut
  into serving pieces

1 tablespoon cooking oil
1 onion, finely chopped
1 green pepper, finely
  chopped
¼ cup water

Drain pineapple. Combine pineapple liquid, soy sauce, ginger, salt, and pepper. Marinate duckling in mixture for at least three hours, turning occasionally.

Remove duckling; pat dry. Reserve marinade. Heat pressure cooker. Add oil; brown duckling. Remove duckling from pressure cooker. Sauté onion and green pepper. Replace duckling. Combine marinade and water. Pour over duckling. Close cover securely. Place pressure regulator on vent pipe. COOK 15 MINUTES. Let pressure drop of its own accord. Thicken sauce, if desired. 4 to 5 servings.

*With the usual long
cooking for tenderness
substantially reduced by
using your pressure cooker —
and a spicy wine sauce —
duck cookery is a breeze.*

WILD DUCK WITH ROSÉ GLAZE

2 wild ducks, about
  1 lb. each
1 teaspoon salt
1 teaspoon soda
  Water
¼ cup dried currants
  Boiling water
1⅓ cups cooked rice
1¼ cups rosé wine
½ teaspoon salt

⅛ teaspoon pepper
⅛ teaspoon nutmeg
⅛ teaspoon allspice
1 teaspoon sugar
¼ cup butter
¼ cup slivered blanched
  almonds
2 tablespoons cooking oil
1 tablespoon lemon juice
½ cup water

Soak ducks several hours in mixture of salt, soda, and
water to cover. Rinse in clear water; wipe dry. Pour
boiling water over currants. Let stand 5 minutes; drain.
Combine currants, rice, ¾ cup wine, salt, pepper,
nutmeg, allspice, and sugar. Let stand 10 minutes.
Melt butter; sauté almonds. Combine with rice mixture.
Stuff lightly into ducks. Heat pressure cooker. Add oil;
brown ducks. Combine remaining ½ cup wine, lemon
juice, and water. Pour over ducks. Close cover
securely. Place pressure regulator on vent pipe.
COOK 25 MINUTES. Cool pressure cooker at once.
Crisp ducks under broiler. 4 servings.

*If you feel that duck is too
fatty or rich, try tender gosling
cooked in tangy orange juice.*

MANDARIN GOSLING

3 lbs. gosling, cut
  into serving pieces
1 tablespoon cooking oil
Salt and pepper
¼ teaspoon sage

1 cup orange juice
2 tablespoons water
1 tablespoon cornstarch
½ cup mandarin orange
  sections

Heat pressure cooker. Add oil; brown gosling.
Pour off drippings. Add salt, pepper, sage, and orange
juice. Close cover securely. Place pressure regulator
on vent pipe. COOK 20 MINUTES. Cool pressure cooker
at once. Remove gosling. Combine water with cornstarch.
Add to liquid in pressure cooker. Heat, stirring
constantly, until gravy has thickened. Add orange
sections; heat through. 3 to 4 servings.

*The distinct lemon flavor comes
from the use of the lemon rind
which is high in flavor oil.*

GOSLING WITH LEMON SAUCE

3 lbs. gosling, cut
  into serving pieces
2 tablespoons cooking oil
½ teaspoon tarragon

½ teaspoon salt
1 cup chicken broth
1 lemon, thinly sliced

Heat pressure cooker. Add oil; brown gosling. Add
remaining ingredients. Close cover securely. Place
pressure regulator on vent pipe. COOK 8 MINUTES.
Cool pressure cooker at once. Thicken sauce, if desired.
3 to 4 servings.

*The sauce is named for
the Cumberland Pass in
Virginia, over which early
settlers traveled.*

PARTRIDGE WITH CUMBERLAND SAUCE

3 lbs. partridge	2 tablespoons orange juice
2 tablespoons cooking oil	2 tablespoons lemon juice
½ teaspoon salt	⅓ cup currant jelly
⅛ teaspoon pepper	2 tablespoons sugar
¼ cup water	

Heat pressure cooker. Add oil; brown partridge.
Combine salt, pepper, water, orange juice, and lemon
juice. Pour over partridge. Close cover securely.
Place pressure regulator on vent pipe. COOK 10
MINUTES. Let pressure drop of its own accord. Place
partridge on warm platter. Add currant jelly and
sugar to sauce in pressure cooker. Heat; stirring
until well blended. Thicken sauce, if desired.
3 to 4 servings.

Variation: If partridge is not available, use 1 pheasant
quartered, or 4 chicken breasts.

*COLONIAL TIMES DINNER
Partridge with Cumberland Sauce
Sweet Potatoes
Creamed Mixed Vegetables
Spoon Bread
Apple Pie with Rum Sauce*

*If quail is not available,
use Cornish game hens for
this delectable dish.*

QUAIL EN CRÉME

2 quail
2 tablespoons cooking oil
1 onion, minced
1 clove garlic, minced
2 whole cloves
4 peppercorns
1 bay leaf
½ teaspoon salt
⅛ teaspoon pepper
Pinch of cayenne pepper
1 teaspoon minced chives
½ cup white wine
1 cup cream

Heat pressure cooker. Add oil; brown quail. Sauté
onion and garlic. Add remaining ingredients, except
cream. Close cover securely. Place pressure regulator
on vent pipe. COOK 10 MINUTES. Let pressure drop of
its own accord. Remove quail from pressure cooker.
Strain liquid. Add cream; heat through. Thicken
sauce, if desired. 2 to 4 servings.

MEETING OF THE GOURMET GROUP
Quail en Créme
Peas steamed with shredded Lettuce
Braised Fine Noodles with Almonds
Whole Strawberries with Sour Cream and Brown Sugar

TURKEY À LA KING

3 lbs. turkey fillets or large chunks
1 teaspoon salt
1 teaspoon Worcestershire sauce
¼ cup chopped green pepper

2 3-ounce cans sliced mushrooms, broiled in butter
½ cup water
2 tablespoons flour
¾ cup cream

Place turkey fillets in pressure cooker. Add salt, Worcestershire sauce, green pepper, mushrooms, and water. Close cover securely. Place pressure regulator on vent pipe. COOK 15 MINUTES. Cool pressure cooker at once. Remove turkey fillets. Combine flour with cream. Add to liquid in pressure cooker. Heat, stirring constantly, until gravy has thickened. Replace turkey; heat through. Serve on hot baking powder biscuits, if desired. 6 to 8 servings.

Ask your butcher to slice the turkey (usually sold frozen) into fillets for you.

TURKEY FILLETS WITH BLACK CHERRY SAUCE

3 lbs. turkey breast, cut into ½-inch thick fillets
2 teaspoons salt
¼ teaspoon pepper
3 tablespoons sugar

1 cup white wine
1½ cups canned pitted black cherries
2 teaspoons cornstarch
2 tablespoons water

Season turkey with salt and pepper. Combine sugar, wine, and black cherries. Pour over turkey in pressure cooker. Close cover securely. Place pressure regulator on vent pipe. COOK 10 MINUTES. Cool pressure cooker at once. Remove turkey. Combine cornstarch with water; add to liquid in pressure cooker. Heat, stirring constantly, until gravy has thickened. Pour over turkey fillets. 6 to 8 servings.

TURKEY IN BURGUNDY WINE

3 lbs. turkey, cut into
serving pieces
½ cup flour
1 teaspoon salt
⅛ teaspoon pepper
2 tablespoons cooking oil
1 onion, sliced

¼ cup sliced celery
1 cup chicken broth
¼ cup mushrooms
2 tablespoons chopped
parsley
⅓ cup Burgundy wine

Dredge turkey with combined flour, salt, and pepper.
Heat pressure cooker. Add oil; brown turkey.
Sauté onion and celery. Add broth, mushrooms, and
parsley. Close cover securely. Place pressure
regulator on vent pipe. COOK 15 MINUTES. Cool
pressure cooker at once. Stir in wine. Thicken sauce,
if desired. 4 to 6 servings.

Variation: To prepare Turkey Au Vin, cousin of
famed Coq Au Vin, add 2 cups whole tiny onions
and ½ pound fresh mushrooms, sliced, in place of
onions, celery, mushrooms, and parsley.

*These boned, rolled roasts
are a boon for working
homemakers.*

TURKEY ROAST

3 lbs. frozen turkey
roast, thawed
1 tablespoon cooking oil
1 onion, finely chopped

½ cup chopped celery
½ teaspoon poultry
seasoning
1 cup water

Heat pressure cooker. Add oil; brown turkey roast.
Add remaining ingredients. Close cover securely.
Place pressure regulator on vent pipe. COOK 20
MINUTES. Let pressure drop of its own accord.
Thicken gravy, if desired. 6 to 8 servings.

DINNER FROM THE FREEZER
Turkey Roast
Frozen Hash Brown Potatoes
Hot Vegetable in Butter Sauce
Thawed Fruit over Ice Cream

SEAFOOD

The fruits of the sea are being enjoyed more and more frequently as cooks discover quick and easy ways like these to prepare low-calorie, low cholesterol seafood.

What could be simpler than shaping a foil bowl, filling it with fish steaks, pouring on wine and pressure cooking it? All in less time than it takes to set the table!

The pages that follow feature the full range of sea fare — crab, halibut, scallops, shrimp, trout — the best gleaned by fishermen on both Coasts and the inland lakes. There are ideas for canned tuna, too, so handy on the kitchen shelf. And be sure to check the index for your favorite seafood to locate other recipes in the soup section and dinner-in-the-cooker section.

*Often overlooked in this
country, carp is popular in
France and Hungary. This
fresh-water fish may
weigh up to 40 pounds, but
is usually 2 to 8 pounds.*

STEAMED CARP

3 lbs. carp, dressed
  Salt and pepper
1 onion, chopped
1 tablespoon parsley

1 bay leaf
3 whole peppercorns
½ cup water

Season carp with salt and pepper; wrap in cheesecloth.
Place in pressure cooker with remaining ingredients.
Close cover securely. Place pressure regulator on
vent pipe. COOK 8 MINUTES. Cool pressure cooker at
once. Drain carp and remove cheesecloth. Serve hot
with lemon wedges or horseradish, if desired. 6 servings.

*Taken from the North Pacific
off Alaska, the king crab is
popular for its tender meat
and distinctive flavor.*

CRAB AU GRATIN

3 lbs. king crab meat,
  cut into chunks
¼ cup butter
½ cup chopped green
  onion

Salt and pepper
¼ cup water
1 cup cream
½ cup grated cheddar
  cheese

Heat pressure cooker. Add butter; sauté crab meat
and onion. Add salt, pepper, and water. Close cover
securely. Place pressure regulator on vent pipe.
COOK 2 MINUTES. Cool pressure cooker at once.
Stir in cream. Turn into a baking dish and top with
grated cheese. Place under broiler until cheese
is bubbly. 10 to 12 servings.

If desired, buttered bread crumbs may be substituted
for the grated cheese. Or, mix the bread crumbs
with the cheese.

Flounder is a flat fish which is much like sole. It is a well-liked, fine, and delicate fish.

BLUE-CHEESED FLOUNDER

2 lbs. flounder fillets	3 tablespoons water
1 tablespoon lemon juice	½ cup cream
1 teaspoon minced onion	⅓ cup crumbled blue
1 teaspoon minced parsley	cheese

Place flounder fillets, lemon juice, onion, parsley, and water in pressure cooker. Close cover securely. Place pressure regulator on vent pipe. COOK 5 MINUTES. Cool pressure cooker at once. Stir in cream and blue cheese. Heat through. 6 to 8 servings.

NUTRITIOUS 'N DELICIOUS
Mermaid Haddie
Baked Potatoes
Country Style Celery (page 177)
Spinach Salad
Broiled Grapefruit

MERMAID HADDIE

2 lbs. haddock fillets	2 tablespoons butter
Salt and pepper	4 slices cooked bacon,
1 3-ounce can sliced	crumbled
mushrooms	½ cup water

Fashion a bowl of heavy duty aluminum foil which will fit loosely in pressure cooker. Place fillets in foil bowl. Sprinkle with salt and pepper. Sauté mushrooms in butter; pour over fillets. Sprinkle bacon on top. Place water, cooking rack, and foil bowl in pressure cooker. Close cover securely. Place pressure regulator on vent pipe. COOK 10 MINUTES. Cool pressure cooker at once. Garnish with lemon slices or wedges, if desired. 6 to 8 servings.

111

FISH MULLIGAN

2 lbs. haddock, cut
into 1-inch pieces
2 cups water
2 cups minced onion
2 cups diced potatoes
⅓ cup rice
⅔ cup minced green
pepper

2 slices cooked bacon,
crumbled
½ cup chopped celery
2 teaspoons salt
¼ teaspoon pepper
2 tablespoons minced
parsley

Combine all ingredients in pressure cooker. Close cover
securely. Place pressure regulator on vent pipe.
COOK 5 MINUTES. Let pressure drop of its own
accord. 6 to 8 servings.

*Serve in large soup bowl, with warm, crusty rolls to be
dunked in the stew. Complete this supper with a tossed
green salad and a refreshing sherbet.*

*Light, souffle-like. Ideal
luncheon for the girls.*

MOLDED HALIBUT WITH LEMON SAUCE

3 cups flaked halibut
¼ cup finely chopped
   onion
2 eggs, beaten
1½ tablespoons cornstarch
¼ teaspoon nutmeg
¼ teaspoon pepper
⅛ teaspoon mace
2 5½-ounce cans
   evaporated milk
1 teaspoon salt
1 cup water
· · · · ·
¼ cup butter
2 tablespoons flour

¼ teaspoon salt
⅛ teaspoon pepper
⅛ teaspoon cayenne
1 cup water
2 tablespoons chopped
   onion
2 peppercorns
1 teaspoon salt
2 sprigs parsley
1 tablespoon lemon juice
2 egg yolks, beaten
   slightly
¼ cup lemon juice
2 tablespoons chopped
   parsley

Thoroughly blend halibut, onion, eggs, cornstarch, nutmeg,
pepper, mace, evaporated milk, and salt. Spoon into
buttered custard cups. Cover with aluminum foil. Place
water, cooking rack, and custard cups in pressure cooker.
Close cover securely. Place pressure regulator on vent
pipe. COOK 15 MINUTES. Cool pressure cooker at once.
In a saucepan, melt butter and stir in flour. Add salt,
pepper, and cayenne. Combine water, onion, peppercorns,
salt, parsley, and lemon juice. Gradually add to flour
mixture, stirring until smooth. Boil 1 minute, stirring
constantly. In a separate bowl, blend together egg yolks,
lemon juice, and ¼ cup boiling mixture. Pour into
saucepan; boil gently until thick and smooth, stirring
constantly. Add parsley. Pour over unmolded halibut.
6 servings.

POOR MAN'S 'LOBSTER'

1 lb. frozen haddock
  fillets, thawed
1 cup water
1 tablespoon salt

1 small potato, peeled
  and halved
1 small onion, quartered

Place haddock and remaining ingredients in pressure cooker. Close cover securely. Place pressure regulator on vent pipe. COOK 3 MINUTES. Cool pressure cooker at once. Drain and serve with melted butter. 4 servings.

Or, chill and use in your favorite salad or as an appetizer.

Variation: Use frozen haddock fillets direct from your freezer. Divide block of fish to fit pressure cooker. COOK 5 MINUTES.

A traditional Norwegian food for smorgasbord and for holiday meals. It is cod treated with lye — the name means "lye fish." The bland white fish is always served with melted butter or with a cream sauce. Add lingonberries or cranberries for color.

LUTEFISK

2 lbs. lutefisk, cut
  into serving pieces
2 cups water
1 teaspoon salt
6 tablespoons butter

¼ cup flour
1 teaspoon salt
1 teaspoon dry mustard
2½ cups milk

Place lutefisk, water, and salt in pressure cooker. Close cover securely. Place pressure regulator on vent pipe. COOK 1 MINUTE. Cool pressure cooker at once. Drain lutefisk and keep warm. Melt butter; blend in flour, salt, and mustard. Add milk, stirring until thickened. Add lutefisk to sauce and heat through. Serve with melted butter and small boiled potatoes, if desired. 6 to 8 servings.

*Serve nutritious salmon often;
it is an excellent source of both
vitamins and minerals.*

DILLY SALMON STEAK

1 tablespoon butter
2 teaspoons finely
   chopped onion
6 salmon steaks,
   ½ inch thick
2 tablespoons lemon juice

1 teaspoon grated
  lemon peel
½ teaspoon dill seed
¼ cup water
½ cup sour cream

Heat pressure cooker. Add butter; sauté onion.
Add salmon steaks, lemon juice, lemon peel, dill seed,
and water. Close cover securely. Place pressure
regulator on vent pipe. COOK 10 MINUTES. Cool
pressure cooker at once. Remove salmon steaks. Blend
sour cream into liquid in pressure cooker. Simmer,
stirring until slightly thickened. Pour sauce over
steaks. 6 servings.

*The easy-to-grow dill with its pretty,
fragrant sprigs need not be limited
to pickle making. Dry the seed (or
buy it) and use it whenever you cook fish.*

SCALLOPED SALMON

3 tablespoons butter
1 tablespoon grated onion
3 tablespoons minced
  green pepper
⅓ cup soft bread crumbs
1 cup milk
1 7¾-ounce can salmon

¾ teaspoon salt
⅛ teaspoon paprika
1 teaspoon Worcestershire
  sauce
2 eggs, beaten
1 cup water

Heat pressure cooker. Melt butter; sauté onion and
pepper. Add remaining ingredients except water.
Spoon into buttered custard cups; cover with
aluminum foil. Place water, cooking rack, and custard
cups in pressure cooker. Close cover securely. Place
pressure regulator on vent pipe. COOK 5 MINUTES.
Cool pressure cooker at once. 4 to 6 servings.

LOBSTER

2 to 3 lbs. lobster	**Salt**
Boiling water	**1 cup water**

Plunge lobster into boiling water to cover; remove.
Place salt, 1 cup water, cooking rack and lobster into
pressure cooker. Close cover securely. Place pressure
regulator on vent pipe. COOK 4 TO 5 MINUTES.
Cool pressure cooker at once. Plunge lobster into
cold water; remove. Crack shell and serve. 2 to 3 servings.

*Cooking fresh lobster is an
exciting experience whether
you choose the large-clawed
Maine lobster or the southern
spiny or rock lobster.*

CURRIED LOBSTER

3 lbs. lobster	**3 tablespoons flour**
Boiling water	**¾ teaspoon salt**
1 cup water	**½ teaspoon curry powder**
2 teaspoons salt	**¼ teaspoon paprika**
3 tablespoons butter	**2 cups milk**
2 tablespoons finely chopped onion	

Plunge lobster into boiling water to cover; remove.
Place 1 cup water, salt, cooking rack, and lobster in
pressure cooker. Close cover securely. Place pressure
regulator on vent pipe. COOK 4 MINUTES. Cool
pressure cooker at once. Plunge lobster into cold water;
remove. Crack shell, remove meat and cut into pieces.
Melt butter; saute' onion. Blend in flour, salt, curry,
and paprika. Add milk; cook until thickened.
Add lobster and heat through. Serve over hot rice,
garnished with chutney, raisins and/or coconut,
if desired. 3 servings.

Variation: Substitute 3 lbs. frozen lobster tails for lobster.
COOK 2 MINUTES. After removing from cold water, cut
away underside membrane and remove meat from shells.

Corn on the Cob (page 178) →

*Who can resist this brilliantly
colored fish, steamed to
tenderness in a wine sauce?*

SALMON STEAK

4 salmon steaks
¼ cup white cooking
   wine
1 tablespoon salad oil

⅛ teaspoon pepper
⅛ teaspoon rosemary
4 slices lemon
½ cup water

Fashion a bowl of heavy duty aluminum foil which will
fit loosely in pressure cooker. Place salmon steaks
in foil bowl. Combine wine, oil, pepper, rosemary,
and lemon slices; pour over fish. Place water,
cooking rack, and foil bowl in pressure cooker. Close
cover securely. Place pressure regulator on vent pipe.
COOK 10 MINUTES. Cool pressure cooker at once.
4 servings.

> *STATE OF WASHINGTON SPECIAL*
> *Salmon Steak or*
> *Dilly Salmon Steak (page 115)*
> *Baked Potatoes with Sour Cream*
> *Mixed Green Salad*
> *Baked Washington Apples*
> *with Caramel Sauce*

SALMON IN BEER SAUCE

4 tablespoons butter
4 tablespoons chopped
   onion
2 cups beer
1 tablespoon sugar
2 cloves

2 teaspoons salt
¼ teaspoon pepper
6 salmon steaks,
   ½ inch thick
2 tablespoons flour
1 tablespoon lemon juice

Heat pressure cooker. Melt butter; sauté onions.
Combine beer, sugar, cloves, salt, and pepper; pour into
pressure cooker. Add salmon. Close cover securely.
Place pressure regulator on vent pipe. COOK 10 MINUTES.
Let pressure drop of its own accord. Remove salmon.
Thicken sauce with flour; add lemon juice. Serve beer
sauce over salmon. 6 servings.

The best scallops are cream-colored, not white. The deep sea scallop is about 1½ inches long and 1 to 1½ inches round. One pound of scallops will serve 2 persons with big appetites and 3 with average capacity.

SCALLOPS

1 lb. scallops　　　　　**½ teaspoon salt**
1 cup water

Place scallops on cooking rack in pressure cooker. Pour combined water and salt over scallops. Close cover securely. Place pressure regulator on vent pipe. Cook as follows: fresh scallops COOK 0 MINUTES; frozen scallops COOK 2 MINUTES. Cool pressure cooker at once. Serve with lemon butter, if desired. 2 to 3 servings.

Teriyaki, whether made with seafood or meat, gets its flavor from the soy sauce. For a sweeter yet stronger soy sauce, try the sauce imported from Japan.

SCALLOPS TERIYAKI

2 lbs. scallops　　　　**2 tablespoons cooking oil**
½ cup soy sauce　　　　**¾ teaspoon ground ginger**
¼ cup cooking sherry　　**1 clove garlic, crushed**
2 tablespoons sugar

Combine all ingredients in pressure cooker. Close cover securely. Place pressure regulator on vent pipe. COOK 0 MINUTES. Cool pressure cooker at once. Place drained scallops on a greased baking pan; broil. Garnish with parsley, if desired. 6 to 8 servings.

SCALLOPS SAUTERNE

1 lb. scallops
1 cup sauterne wine
1 teaspoon chicken bouillon

½ teaspoon salt
¼ cup grated mild Cheddar cheese

Place scallops in pressure cooker. Combine wine, chicken bouillon, and salt; pour over scallops. Close cover securely. Place pressure regulator on vent pipe. Cook as follows: fresh scallops COOK 0 MINUTES; frozen scallops COOK 2 MINUTES. Cool pressure cooker at once. Thicken sauce, if desired. Garnish with grated cheese. 4 servings.

LITTLE DINNER FOR FOUR
Consomme Madrilene
Scallops Sauterne
Asparagus Spears   Romaine Salad
Crescent Rolls
Chocolate Torte

The French call scallops "Coquilles Saint Jacques" and serve them a variety of ways.

SCALLOPS PROVENCALE

3 tablespoons olive oil
4 shallots, sliced
1 clove garlic, minced
6 tomatoes, peeled and quartered
1 tablespoon chopped parsley
½ teaspoon salt

⅛ teaspoon white pepper
½ teaspoon thyme
½ teaspoon oregano
¼ cup water
2 lbs. scallops
½ lb. mushrooms
2 teaspoons lemon juice

Heat pressure cooker. Add olive oil; sauté shallots and garlic. Add tomatoes, parsley, salt, pepper, thyme, oregano, and water. Close cover securely. Place pressure regulator on vent pipe. COOK 5 MINUTES. Cool pressure cooker at once. Add remaining ingredients. Close cover securely. Place pressure regulator on vent pipe. COOK 0 MINUTES. Cool pressure cooker at once. Thicken sauce, if desired. 6 to 8 servings.

If you have a little garden spot, order some seed and grow your own pea pods for this and other Chinese specialties. They grow easily and a bumper crop can be frozen for winter use.

SWEET-SOUR SHRIMP

1 lb. shrimp, peeled and cleaned	3 tablespoons vinegar
½ lb. Chinese pea pods	⅔ cup pineapple juice
2 tablespoons soy sauce	3 tablespoons sugar
	1 cup chicken broth

Combine all ingredients in pressure cooker. Close cover securely. Place pressure regulator on vent pipe. COOK 2 MINUTES. Cool pressure cooker at once. Thicken sauce, if desired, and serve on hot rice. 4 servings.

*Take your family table traveling
on a trip to romantic India.
Enjoy curry and condiments
amidst talk of the Gandhis and
the Taj Mahal.*

SHRIMP CURRY

2 tablespoons butter
¼ cup chopped onion
¼ cup sliced mushrooms
½ teaspoon curry powder
½ teaspoon salt
⅛ teaspoon pepper

1 lb. shrimp, peeled
    and cleaned
4 lemon slices
1 cup bouillon
3 tablespoons flour
1 cup milk

Heat pressure cooker. Add butter; sauté onion and
mushrooms. Add curry powder, salt, pepper, shrimp,
lemon, and bouillon. Close cover securely. Place
pressure regulator on vent pipe. COOK 2 MINUTES.
Cool pressure cooker at once. Combine flour with milk.
Add to liquid in pressure cooker. Heat, stirring
constantly until sauce has thickened. If desired, serve
over rice with a selection of condiments (see below).
4 servings.

*How many "boys" for your curry? When India was part of
the British Empire, a different servant boy carried each
condiment to guests at a curry dinner. Choose: raisins,
toasted coconut, chopped hard-cooked eggs, chutney, salted
peanuts or almonds, crumbled bacon, or diced tomatoes.*

SHRIMP IN PATTY SHELLS

1½ lbs. shrimp,
   peeled and cleaned
¼ cup chopped green
   onion
3 tablespoons butter
Dash cayenne pepper

⅓ cup dry white wine
2 tablespoons flour
1 cup milk
6 patty shells
½ cup shredded sharp
   American cheese

Heat pressure cooker. Add butter; sauté shrimp and onion. Add pepper and wine. Close cover securely. Place pressure regulator on vent pipe. COOK 2 MINUTES. Cool pressure cooker at once. Blend flour into milk. Add to shrimp and cook until thickened. Spoon into patty shells. Top with cheese. 6 servings.

A SPECIAL LUNCHEON
Shrimp in Patty Shells
Tomato Aspic
garnished with olives
Tiny Butter Rolls
Tri-color Sherbet Cups
Coconut Macaroons

SHRIMP ROYALE

⅓ cup butter
½ cup coconut flakes
¼ cup fine bread crumbs
3 tablespoons chopped
   parsley
3 garlic cloves, minced
¾ teaspoon salt

¼ teaspoon paprika
⅛ teaspoon cayenne
   pepper
2 lbs. shrimp, shelled
   and cleaned
½ cup sherry

Heat pressure cooker. Add butter; sauté mixture of coconut flakes, bread crumbs, parsley, garlic, salt, paprika, and pepper. Remove approximately ¼ cup of mixture for topping. Add shrimp; toss gently. Add sherry. Close cover securely. Place pressure regulator on vent pipe. COOK 1 MINUTE. Cool pressure cooker at once. Garnish with reserved topping mixture. Broil a few seconds, if desired. 6 servings.

If desired, coconut may be omitted and bread crumbs increased to ¾ cup.

*If sole is not available, this
recipe may be used with any
white fish — halibut, pike
or haddock.*

FILLET OF SOLE

1 lb. sole fillets	1½ teaspoons
2 tablespoons butter	Worcestershire sauce
Salt and pepper	½ teaspoon dry mustard
¾ cup beer	

Heat pressure cooker; melt butter. Sprinkle sole with
salt and pepper; place in pressure cooker. Combine
remaining ingredients; pour over fish. Close cover
securely. Place pressure regulator on vent pipe.
COOK 10 MINUTES. Let pressure drop of its own accord.
Thicken sauce, if desired. 4 servings.

Variation: Drain sole on absorbent paper, chill and
serve on crackers as an appetizer.

*Another classic French seafood
specialty, which has been
introduced to Americans by
French restaurants. Sole is a
supremely delicate fish.*

SOLE WITH GRAPE SAUCE

2 lbs. sole fillets	¾ cup cream
¾ cup sauterne wine	¾ cup seedless green
½ teaspoon salt	grapes, halved
3 teaspoons cornstarch	

Wrap sole fillets in cheesecloth. Place wine, cooking
rack, and sole in pressure cooker. Close cover securely.
Place pressure regulator on vent pipe. COOK 5 MINUTES.
Cool pressure cooker at once. Remove fish, sprinkle
with salt and keep warm. Combine cornstarch with cream.
Add to wine in pressure cooker. Heat, stirring
constantly until sauce has thickened. Add grapes and
heat through. Pour sauce over fillets. 6 to 8 servings.

STUFFED TROUT

3 tablespoons butter	¼ cup water
¼ cup diced celery	. . . . .
¼ cup diced green pepper	3 lbs. trout
2 tablespoons chopped onion	2 tablespoons barbecue sauce
1½ cups seasoned croutons	½ cup water

Heat pressure cooker. Add butter; sauté celery, pepper, and onion. Toss with croutons and water. Stuff trout loosely with mixture. Brush trout with barbecue sauce; wrap in cheesecloth. Place water, cooking rack, and trout in pressure cooker. Close cover securely. Place pressure regulator on vent pipe. COOK 8 MINUTES. Cool pressure cooker at once. Serve with barbecue sauce, if desired. 6 to 8 servings.

TROUT TREAT
Tomato Bouillon
Stuffed Trout
Hot Cabbage Slaw
Parmesan French Bread
Lemon Tarts

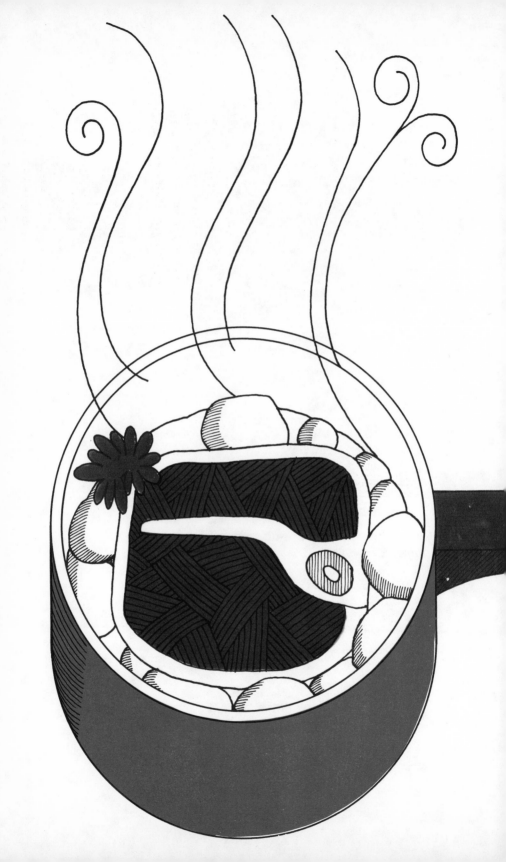

DINNER IN THE COOKER

For convenience in cooking, simplicity of service, and excellence in eating, nothing surpasses a dinner main dish from the pressure cooker.

Choose meat, poultry, or seafood, skillfully combined with a complementary vegetable or starch, all calculated to save you work, time, and dishwashing. To these pressure cooker dinners you need add only a salad and dessert — maybe a bread — for a satisfying menu.

Turn to this chapter often if you live in a warm climate or during the hot months of summer, for these recipes will give you much the same blending of flavors and eating quality of casseroles baked in the oven — without either the oven heat or time.

A unique service — six dinners for twosomes featuring three foods cooked at one time — is also part of this chapter.

Whether it is a ragout (French for stew), a scallop (English for casserole), or a pilaf (Turkish for rice dish), dinner in the pressure cooker can be translated: American for great eating.

Downright good eating.

BEEF STEW 'N NUTMEG DUMPLINGS

2 lbs. beef, cut into
  1-inch pieces
1 tablespoon cooking oil
1 clove garlic, cut in half
1½ cups water
⅛ teaspoon thyme
3 teaspoons salt
⅛ teaspoon pepper
2 bay leaves
1 cup cut green beans
1 cup peas
2 onions, chopped

2 carrots, cut into
  ¼-inch slices
. . . . .
1½ cups sifted flour
4 teaspoons baking
  powder
½ teaspoon salt
½ teaspoon nutmeg
1 tablespoon shortening
1 egg, beaten
⅔ cup milk

Heat pressure cooker. Add oil; brown beef and garlic. Remove garlic. Stir in water, thyme, salt, pepper, and bay leaves. Close cover securely. Place pressure regulator on vent pipe. COOK 15 MINUTES. Cool pressure cooker at once. Remove bay leaves. Stir in vegetables.

Sift flour, baking powder, salt, and nutmeg. Cut in shortening, until mixture is crumbly. Combine egg and milk; add to dry ingredients. Stir just until moistened. Drop from tablespoon on bubbling stew. Remove sealing ring from cover. Place cover loosely on pressure cooker without pressure regulator. STEAM 15 MINUTES. 6 to 8 servings.

Variation: Use 1½ cups packaged biscuit mix following dumpling recipe and adding ½ teaspoon nutmeg.

STEW FOR SUPPER
Beef Stew 'n Nutmeg Dumplings
Lettuce with Thousand Island Dressing
Blueberry Pie with Ice Cream

MEATBALLS WITH ONION RICE

½ lb. ground pork
½ lb. ground beef
1½ slices white bread
½ cup chopped onion
1 clove garlic, minced
1 teaspoon salt
¼ teaspoon pepper
⅛ teaspoon cayenne pepper
½ teaspoon salad herbs
1 egg, beaten

1 cup fine dry bread crumbs
¾ cup chopped parsley
2 tablespoons cooking oil
1 cup chopped onion
1 cup rice
2 cups water
2 teaspoons instant beef bouillon
1 teaspoon salt

Combine pork and beef with bread which has been dipped in water and pressed dry. Add next seven ingredients; mix well. Form into 10 meatballs. Blend bread crumbs with parsley. Roll meatballs in crumb mixture. Chill. Heat pressure cooker. Add oil; brown meatballs. Remove meatballs from pressure cooker. Sauté onion. Add remaining ingredients; stir. Place meatballs in pressure cooker. Close cover securely. Place pressure regulator on vent pipe. COOK 0 MINUTES. Let pressure drop of its own accord. 4 to 6 servings.

Tired of hamburgers? Use budget-beating ground beef to stuff a cabbage.

STUFFED WHOLE CABBAGE

2 lb. head of cabbage
1 lb. ground beef, cooked
1 cup cooked rice
1 onion, minced
¼ cup chopped celery

1 teaspoon salt
¼ teaspoon pepper
1 cup beef bouillon
½ cup water

Hollow out cabbage from top, leaving thick shell. Combine beef, rice, onion, celery, salt, pepper, and bouillon. Stuff cabbage. Cover top with cabbage leaves, secured by toothpicks. Place water, cooking rack, and cabbage in pressure cooker. Do not fill over ⅔ full. Close cover securely. Place pressure regulator on vent pipe. COOK 10 MINUTES. Cool pressure cooker at once. 4 to 6 servings.

MEXICAN BRAISED LIVER

1 lb. liver, cut into
  serving pieces
¼ cup flour
4 tablespoons bacon
  drippings
½ teaspoon salt

⅛ teaspoon pepper
3 carrots, diced
1 green pepper, sliced
3 small onions
½ cup water

Dredge liver with flour. Heat pressure cooker. Add
bacon drippings; brown liver. Season with salt and
pepper. Place cooking rack over liver. Arrange carrots,
green pepper, and onions on rack. Add water. Close
cover securely. Place pressure regulator on vent pipe.
COOK 5 MINUTES. Cool pressure cooker at once.
Arrange vegetables in mounds on pieces of liver.
4 servings.

VERMONT CORNED BEEF

2 lbs. corned beef
Water
. . . . .
1 cup water
5 small potatoes

1 cup sliced rutabaga
3 carrots, cut into
1-inch pieces
1 lb. cabbage, cut
into wedges

Cover corned beef with cold water; soak for one hour.
Drain. Place 1 cup water, cooking rack, and corned beef
in pressure cooker. Close cover securely. Place
pressure regulator on vent pipe. COOK 40 MINUTES.
Cool pressure cooker at once. Add vegetables.
Do not fill pressure cooker over ⅔ full. Close cover
securely. Place pressure regulator on vent pipe.
COOK 5 MINUTES. Cool pressure cooker at once.
6 to 8 servings.

COMPANY CORNED BEEF

4 lbs. corned beef brisket
Water
. . . . .
2 small oranges, sliced
2 small onions, sliced
2 cloves garlic, chopped

1½ cups sliced celery
1 tablespoon dill seed
2 bay leaves
4 cinnamon sticks
2 cups water

Cover corned beef with cold water; soak for one hour.
Drain. Place corned beef in pressure cooker. Combine
remaining ingredients; pour over corned beef. Close
cover securely. Place pressure regulator on vent pipe.
COOK 50 MINUTES. (If less tender cut is used, cook
additional 10 minutes.) Let pressure drop of its own accord.
Serve with mustard sauce, if desired. 6 to 8 servings.

Mustard Sauce

Melt 2 tablespoons butter in top of double boiler.
Stir in 1 tablespoon flour, 1 teaspoon salt, ⅛ teaspoon
white pepper, 1 to 2 tablespoons prepared mustard.
Beat 1 egg yolk with ⅔ cup milk; stir into flour mixture.
Cook and stir about 5 minutes, or until thickened and
smooth. Blend in 1 tablespoon lemon juice just
before serving.

A highly nutritious dish.

STEAK AND BROWN RICE DINNER

2 lbs. round steak, cut
into serving pieces
2 tablespoons olive oil
½ cup brown rice

3 cups water
1 package dry onion soup
1 10-ounce package frozen
Italian green beans

Heat pressure cooker. Add oil; brown meat. Remove
meat from pressure cooker. Add remaining ingredients;
stir well. Place meat in pressure cooker. Close cover
securely. Place pressure regulator on vent pipe.
COOK 15 MINUTES. Let pressure drop of its own
accord. Remove meat. Fluff rice mixture with a fork
while steaming. 4 to 6 servings.

HEARTY AND HEALTHY
Cube Steak Supper
Lettuce Wedges with Cucumber Dressing
Whole Wheat Rolls
Apricot Cobbler

CUBE STEAK SUPPER

4 cube steaks
¼ teaspoon salt
Pepper
2 tablespoons flour
½ cup bread crumbs
⅛ teaspoon poultry
seasoning
½ teaspoon minced onion

1 tablespoon melted
butter
1 tablespoon water
1 tablespoon cooking oil
⅔ cup rice
3½ cups stewed tomatoes
¼ teaspoon salt

Roll steaks in mixture of ¼ teaspoon salt, pepper,
and flour. Combine crumbs, poultry seasoning, onion,
butter, and water. Place a fourth of the stuffing on each
steak. Fold steaks over stuffing; fasten with skewers or
toothpicks. Heat pressure cooker. Add oil; sear rolled
steak. Add rice, tomatoes, and ¼ teaspoon salt. Close
cover securely. Place pressure regulator on vent pipe.
COOK 10 MINUTES. Let pressure drop of its own accord.
4 servings.

For the sailor to prepare for himself and his mate in the galley. Or for a smart sailor's wife to prepare ahead.

SAILOR'S STEW

2 lbs. beef, cut into 1-inch squares
2 tablespoons cooking oil
1 cup chopped onion
1½ teaspoon salt
½ teaspoon pepper
½ teaspoon marjoram
1½ cups beer
4 potatoes, cut into halves

Heat pressure cooker. Add oil; brown meat. Sauté onions. Add remaining ingredients. Close cover securely. Place pressure regulator on vent pipe. COOK 15 MINUTES. Cool pressure cooker at once. 4 to 6 servings.

*A winter main dish to warm
the cockles of your family's
heart . . . protein-rich.*

BEEF 'N BEAN PLATTER

3 lbs. rolled boneless
  pot roast
2 tablespoons shortening
1 10¾-ounce can
  condensed tomato soup
1 soup can water

1 large bay leaf
¼ teaspoon garlic powder
2 10½-ounce packages
  frozen lima beans
½ cup sliced stuffed olives

Heat pressure cooker. Add shortening; brown roast on
all sides. Remove excess drippings. Add next four
ingredients. Close cover securely. Place pressure
regulator on vent pipe. COOK 1 HOUR. Let pressure
drop of its own accord. Remove bay leaf. Add lima
beans and olives. Close cover securely. Place
pressure regulator on vent pipe. COOK 2 MINUTES.
Cool pressure cooker at once. Thicken sauce, if desired.
8 to 10 servings.

*The French skill in combining
meat and vegetables and
cooking them with wine and
herbs . . . readily adaptable to
pressure cookery.*

BEEF MONTPARNASSE

2 lbs. round steak, cut
  into serving pieces
2 tablespoons shortening
2 slices bacon, crumbled
6 small white onions
6 new potatoes, peeled
2 3-ounce cans mushrooms
  with liquid

½ cup dry white wine
1 tablespoon minced
  parsley
2 teaspoons salt
½ teaspoon pepper
1 bay leaf

Heat pressure cooker. Add shortening; brown steak.
Add remaining ingredients. Close cover securely. Place
pressure regulator on vent pipe. COOK 15 MINUTES.
Let pressure drop of its own accord. Remove bay leaf.
Thicken gravy, if desired. 6 servings.

COLLOPS OF VEAL

1½ lbs. veal, cut into
   1-inch cubes
2 tablespoons shortening
2 chicken bouillon cubes
1½ cups boiling water
2 cups finely chopped
   celery

½ cup rice
2 onions, finely chopped
2 tablespoons soy sauce
1 10½-ounce can cream
   of mushroom soup
Chow mein noodles

Heat pressure cooker. Add shortening; brown veal.
Dissolve chicken bouillon cubes in boiling water.
Combine chicken bouillon, celery, rice, onions, soy sauce,
and cream of mushroom soup. Pour over veal; stir.
Close cover securely. Place pressure regulator on vent
pipe. COOK 20 MINUTES. Cool pressure cooker at
once. Serve over chow mein noodles. 6 servings.

CHICKEN 'N RICE WITH CREAM GRAVY

3 lbs. chicken, cut into
   serving pieces
2 tablespoons lemon juice
2 teaspoons salt
1 teaspoon paprika
¼ teaspoon white pepper
1 cup sifted flour
3 tablespoons cooking oil
¼ teaspoon rosemary

½ cup water
1 cup rice
2 cups water
1 teaspoon salt

. . . . .
1 10½-ounce can
   condensed cream
   of mushroom soup
1 cup sour cream

Sprinkle chicken with lemon juice. Set aside for 15
minutes. Dredge chicken in combined salt, paprika,
pepper, and flour. Heat pressure cooker. Add oil;
brown chicken. Sprinkle with rosemary. Add water.
Close cover securely. Place pressure regulator on
vent pipe. COOK 8 MINUTES. Cool pressure cooker
at once. Add rice, water, and salt. Close cover securely.
Place pressure regulator on vent pipe. COOK 0 MINUTES.
Let pressure drop of its own accord. Place rice on
warm platter in a mound; surround with chicken.
Spoon mushroom soup into pressure cooker. Mix until
smooth. Gradually add sour cream, mixing well.
Heat through. Pour over chicken and rice.
4 to 6 servings.

Let the main dish set your meal-time mood. Hawaiian, of course.

CHINESE CHICKEN ALMOND

3 lbs. chicken, cut into serving pieces
2 tablespoons shortening
½ cup water
½ cup diced onion
½ cup diced celery
1 3-ounce can sliced mushrooms, drained

1 cup rice
1½ cups bean sprouts
1 8-ounce can water chestnuts, sliced
2 tablespoons soy sauce
1½ cups chicken broth
½ cup toasted slivered almonds

Heat pressure cooker. Add shortening; brown chicken. Add water. Close cover securely. Place pressure regulator on vent pipe. COOK 8 MINUTES. Cool pressure cooker at once. Remove chicken. Stir in remaining ingredients, except almonds. Return chicken to pressure cooker. Close cover securely. Place pressure regulator on vent pipe. COOK 0 MINUTES. Let pressure drop of its own accord. To serve, sprinkle with almonds. Pass soy sauce, if desired. 4 to 6 servings.

INDIA CHICKEN

3½ lbs. chicken, cut into serving pieces
Paprika
2 tablespoons cooking oil
2 onions, chopped
2 teaspoons salt
¼ teaspoon pepper
¼ teaspoon ground cloves

¼ teaspoon ginger
¼ teaspoon cinnamon
¼ teaspoon mace
½ teaspoon saffron
2 tablespoons raisins
½ cup rice
2 cups water

Sprinkle chicken lightly with paprika. Heat pressure cooker. Add oil; brown chicken. Combine seasonings, raisins, and rice. Place alternate layers of chicken and rice mixture into pressure cooker, beginning with chicken and ending with rice. Pour water over chicken. Close cover securely. Place pressure regulator on vent pipe. COOK 15 MINUTES. Let pressure drop of its own accord. 4 to 6 servings.

A Middle Eastern specialty.

CHICKEN PILAU

3 lbs. chicken, cut into
  serving pieces
2 tablespoons shortening
1 onion, sliced
1 clove garlic, minced
2 cups chicken broth

2 teaspoons salt
¼ teaspoon ground ginger
1 teaspoon curry powder
1 cup rice
1 cup yogurt

Heat pressure cooker. Add shortening; brown chicken.
Remove chicken; sauté onion and garlic. Stir in broth,
salt, ginger, curry powder, and rice. Place chicken in
pressure cooker. Close cover securely. Place pressure
regulator on vent pipe. COOK 10 MINUTES. Let
pressure drop of its own accord. Remove chicken.
Stir yogurt into rice mixture; let stand five minutes.
4 to 6 servings.

*No food from across the sea has
found such favor in the United
States as Italy's spaghetti sauce
and spaghetti.*

CHICKEN IN SPAGHETTI SAUCE

3 lbs. chicken, cut into
  serving pieces
2 tablespoons cooking oil
1 cup chopped onion
1 cup sliced celery
1 cup sliced carrot
2 cups stewed tomatoes

1 6-ounce can tomato
  paste
½ cup dry white wine
2 teaspoons salt
½ teaspoon pepper
2 whole cloves
⅛ teaspoon cinnamon

Heat pressure cooker. Add oil; brown chicken. Remove
chicken. Sauté onion, celery, and carrots. Stir in
tomatoes, tomato paste, wine, salt, pepper, cloves, and
cinnamon. Place chicken in pressure cooker. Close
cover securely. Place pressure regulator on vent pipe.
COOK 10 MINUTES. Cool pressure cooker at once.
Serve with spaghetti, if desired. 4 to 6 servings.

CHICKEN AL FRESCO

3 lbs. chicken,
  cut into quarters
¼ cup cooking oil
1 onion, chopped
1 green pepper, chopped
1 clove garlic, minced
3 whole cloves
1 bay leaf

¼ teaspoon oregano
1 teaspoon chili powder
½ teaspoon pepper
1 teaspoon salt
½ cup water
. . . . .
2 tomatoes, quartered
1 cup sliced stuffed olives

Heat pressure cooker. Add oil; brown chicken. Combine next 10 ingredients; pour over chicken. Close cover securely. Place pressure regulator on vent pipe. COOK 10 MINUTES. Cool pressure cooker at once. Place chicken on heated platter. Stir tomatoes and olives into sauce; heat through. Thicken sauce, if desired. 4 to 6 servings.

CHICKEN WITH ALMOND NOODLES

2 tablespoons butter
2 cups chopped celery
3 onions, sliced
1 cup mushrooms
2 lbs. boned chicken, cut
  into strips
2 cups chicken broth
1 teaspoon salt

¼ teaspoon pepper
2 tablespoons cornstarch
¼ cup water
2 teaspoons soy sauce
½ cup slivered almonds
2½ cups chow mein
  noodles

Heat pressure cooker. Add butter; sauté celery, onions, and mushrooms. Stir in chicken, chicken broth, salt, and pepper. Close cover securely. Place pressure regulator on vent pipe. COOK 5 MINUTES. Cool pressure cooker at once. Blend cornstarch and water. Stir into chicken mixture. Cook until thickened, stirring constantly. Season with soy sauce. Spoon chicken onto large serving plate. Surround with a ring of combined almonds and noodles. 6 to 8 servings.

Chicken once a week is a good bet for the budget.

CHICKEN AND FRESH VEGETABLES

3 lbs. chicken, cut into
  serving pieces
1 tablespoon shortening
  Salt and pepper
6 small white onions
3 ribs celery, chopped
½ cup water

½ green pepper, cut
  into strips
1 cup snap beans, cut
  into 1-inch pieces
1 cup green peas
½ cup pimiento strips

Heat pressure cooker. Add shortening; brown chicken.
Season with salt and pepper. Add onions, celery, and
water. Close cover securely. Place pressure regulator on
vent pipe. COOK 10 MINUTES. Cool pressure cooker
at once. Add remaining ingredients. Close cover securely.
Place pressure regulator on vent pipe. COOK 1 MINUTE.
Let pressure drop of its own accord. Thicken gravy,
if desired. 4 to 6 servings.

WHEN THE PRESSURE'S ON
Chicken with Fresh Vegetables or
Chicken-Lima Dinner
Wilted Lettuce
Brown 'n Serve French Rolls
Fruit Turnovers

CHICKEN-LIMA DINNER

3 lbs. chicken, cut into
  serving pieces
1 tablespoon cooking oil
1 cup rice
2 tablespoons butter, melted
1 cup finely chopped onion

1 tablespoon parsley
1 teaspoon marjoram
3 cups chicken broth
1 10-ounce package
  frozen lima beans
1½ teaspoons salt

Heat pressure cooker. Add oil; brown chicken.
Remove chicken. Combine remaining ingredients in
pressure cooker. Place chicken in pressure cooker.
Close cover securely. Place pressure regulator on
vent pipe. COOK 15 MINUTES. Cool pressure cooker
at once. 4 to 6 servings.

CLUB CHICKEN

1 tablespoon cooking oil
¼ cup diced onion
1 4-ounce can mushroom stems and pieces, drained
2 cups cubed cooked chicken
¼ cup chopped celery
2 tablespoons minced parsley

1 cup rice
1 tablespoon chopped pimiento
1½ cups water
1 teaspoon instant chicken bouillon
½ teaspoon salt
⅛ teaspoon thyme
⅛ teaspoon pepper

Heat pressure cooker. Add oil; sauté onions and mushrooms. Add remaining ingredients. Close cover securely. Place pressure regulator on vent pipe. COOK 0 MINUTES. Let pressure drop of its own accord. 4 to 6 servings.

LUNCH FOR THE COMMITTEE MEETING
Club Chicken
Frozen Fruit Salad
Hot Rolls
Assorted Bar Cookies

In Germany and Austria, poultry and sauerkraut are popular meal mates. The Viennese stuff birds with kraut.

DUCK WITH KRAUT

3 lbs. duck, cut into serving pieces
Salt and pepper
1 tablespoon cooking oil

1 clove garlic
2½ cups sauerkraut
1 tablespoon sugar
½ cup water

Remove as much fat as possible from duck. Season with salt and pepper. Heat pressure cooker. Add oil and garlic clove; brown duck. Pour off excess fat. Remove duck and garlic clove. Add sauerkraut, sugar, and water. Replace duck. Close cover securely. Place pressure regulator on vent pipe. COOK 15 MINUTES. Let pressure drop of its own accord. 4 servings.

LAMB STEW WITH POTATO DUMPLINGS

3 tablespoons flour	2 ribs celery, cut into
1½ teaspoons salt	2-inch pieces
¼ teaspoon pepper	1¾ cups water
2 lbs. boned lamb	1 tablespoon
shoulder, cut into	Worcestershire sauce
1-inch cubes	. . . . .
2 tablespoons shortening	1 egg
6 carrots, cut into	1 cup water
1-inch pieces	½ cup potato pancake mix
3 onions, cut into quarters	⅓ cup dry bread crumbs

Combine flour, salt, and pepper. Dredge lamb cubes.
Heat pressure cooker. Add shortening; brown lamb. Stir
in carrots, onions, celery, water, and Worcestershire sauce.
Close cover securely. Place pressure regulator on vent
pipe. COOK 8 MINUTES. Cool pressure cooker at once.

Combine egg, water, and pancake mix; let stand 10
minutes. Stir in dry bread. Drop from tablespoon on
bubbling stew. Remove sealing ring from cover. Place
cover loosely on pressure cooker without pressure
regulator. STEAM 10 MINUTES. 4 to 6 servings.

ST. PATRICK'S DAY DINNER
Lamb Stew with Potato Dumplings
or Lamb Fricassee with Carrots
Green-tinted Pear Salad
Shamrock Biscuits
Lemon Ice with Mint Sauce
Irish Coffee

LAMB FRICASSEE WITH CARROTS

2 lbs. boneless lamb
stew meat, cut into
1-inch cubes
2 tablespoons cooking oil
1½ cups sliced carrots
3 onions, sliced

2 teaspoons salt
¼ teaspoon pepper
1 teaspoon dried mint
flakes or 1 tablespoon
fresh mint leaves
1 cup water

Heat pressure cooker. Add oil; brown meat. Drain off
excess drippings. Add remaining ingredients. Close
cover securely. Place pressure regulator on vent pipe.
COOK 5 MINUTES. Cool pressure cooker at once.
Thicken gravy, if desired. 6 to 8 servings.

*Lamb is the principal meat of
Greece where it may be broiled
over an open fire, cut up for
tasty stews, or combine with
eggplant for the national
favorite, moussaka.*

STUFFED PEPPERS A LA GRECQUE

4 slices bacon, diced
½ lb. ground lamb
¼ cup chopped onion
½ cup cooked rice
1 egg, beaten
⅛ teaspoon poultry
seasoning

¼ teaspoon salt
⅛ teaspoon pepper
4 green peppers, cored
1 cup water

Brown bacon, lamb, and onion. Pour off excess drippings.
Combine bacon, lamb, onion, rice, egg, poultry
seasonings, salt, and pepper. Stuff the peppers. Place
water, cooking rack, and peppers in pressure cooker.
Close cover securely. Place pressure regulator on vent
pipe. COOK 3 MINUTES. Cool pressure cooker at once.
4 servings.

Variation: Beef-stuffed Peppers: Follow recipe above
stuffing peppers with mixture of ½ lb. ground round,
browned, 1 cup cooked rice, ¼ cup each chopped red
and green pepper, and ¼ cup chopped onion.

For a stew-pendous supper.

MINTED LAMB AND VEGETABLE POT

2 tablespoons shortening
1½ pounds lamb, cut into 1-inch cubes
1 10¾-ounce can condensed cream of chicken soup
¼ cup mint jelly
1 teaspoon rosemary, crushed
½ cup water
2 lbs. rutabaga, cut into eight wedges
1 10-ounce package frozen peas
½ cup water

Heat pressure cooker. Add shortening; brown lamb. Stir in soup, jelly, rosemary, water, and rutabaga. Close cover securely. Place pressure regulator on vent pipe. COOK 12 MINUTES. Cool pressure cooker at once. Add peas; bring to boil. SIMMER 5 MINUTES without cover. Thicken sauce, if desired. 4 to 6 servings.

LAMB CURRY

2 lbs. lamb stew meat, cut into 1-inch cubes
1 tablespoon cooking oil
2 cubes chicken bouillon
1 cup boiling water
1 6-ounce can tomato paste
2 teaspoons curry powder
1 teaspoon salt
½ teaspoon sugar
¼ teaspoon pepper
1 teaspoon Worcestershire sauce
1/16 teaspoon each cinnamon, nutmeg, cloves, allspice, and chili powder
2 tart apples, peeled and diced
1 large onion, diced
1 clove garlic, minced
¼ cup raisins
½ cup coconut
1 slice lemon

Heat pressure cooker. Add oil; brown meat. Add remaining ingredients; mix well. Close cover securely. Place pressure regulator on vent pipe. COOK 10 MINUTES. Cool pressure cooker at once. Serve over broad noodles or white rice, if desired. 6 to 8 servings.

Stick-to-the-ribs fare.

BRAISED PORK ROAST WITH KIDNEY BEANS

2 cups dried kidney
  beans
¼ cup cooking oil
1 tablespoon salt
  Water
  . . . . .
1½ lbs. boned pork
  shoulder roast
1 teaspoon salt

¼ teaspoon pepper
2 tablespoons cooking oil
1 onion, chopped
½ green pepper, chopped
2 tablespoons brown
  sugar
1 teaspoon dry mustard
2½ cups mixed vegetable
  juice

Wash dried beans; soak overnight in oil, salt, and
enough water to cover completely. Drain; discard
liquid. Rub pork roast with salt and pepper. Heat
pressure cooker. Add oil; brown roast. Add kidney
beans and remaining ingredients. Close cover securely.
Place pressure regulator on vent pipe. COOK 25
MINUTES. Let pressure drop of its own accord.
6 servings.

CARIBBEAN RICE

1 lb. link pork sausages,
  cut in half
1 onion, chopped
1 green pepper, chopped
1 clove garlic, minced

1 6-ounce can tomato
  paste
2 cups water
1 teaspoon salt
½ teaspoon oregano
1 cup rice

Heat pressure cooker. Brown pork sausages; pour
off excess fat. Sauté onion, green pepper, and garlic.
Combine tomato paste and water. Pour into pressure
cooker. Stir in remaining ingredients. Close cover
securely. Place pressure regulator on vent pipe.
COOK 0 MINUTES. Let pressure drop of its own accord.
Stir gently with a fork. 4 servings.

POTATO-HAM SCALLOP SUPREME

1 lb. cooked ham, cut into
   1-inch cubes
1 tablespoon cooking oil
4 cups sliced potatoes
1 onion, chopped

1 10-ounce can
   condensed cream
   of celery soup
1¼ cups milk
  2 teaspoons salt
  ⅛ teaspoon pepper

Heat pressure cooker. Add oil; brown ham. Remove
from heat; stir in potatoes and onion. Combine
soup, milk, salt, and pepper; pour over potatoes.
Close cover securely. Place pressure regulator on vent
pipe. COOK 3 MINUTES. Cool pressure cooker at
once. Garnish with hot asparagus spears, if desired.
4 to 6 servings.

Variation: Substitute 12-ounce can pork luncheon meat,
cubed, for ham.

Bundles of good eating.

HAM CABBAGE ROLLS

1 head of cabbage
  Hot water
2 cups chopped cooked
  ham
1 cup cooked rice
1 onion, minced

½ teaspoon dry mustard
1 teaspoon salt
¼ teaspoon pepper
1 cup tomato juice
2 tablespoons cooking oil

Dip cabbage leaves in hot water; dry on a towel.
Combine ham, rice, onion, mustard, salt, pepper, and
¼ cup tomato juice. Place a tablespoon of meat mixture
onto each leaf. Roll leaf around mixture; fasten with a
toothpick. Heat pressure cooker. Add oil; brown rolls.
Add remaining ¾ cup tomato juice. Close cover
securely. Place pressure regulator on vent pipe.
COOK 10 MINUTES. Let pressure drop of its own accord.
4 to 6 servings.

Variation: Substitute 1 pound ground beef, well browned,
for cooked ham.

CREAMY HAM 'N PEAS

½ lb. cooked ham, cubed
2 tablespoons cooking oil
1½ lbs. fresh peas or
  2 10-ounce packages
  frozen peas

½ teaspoon curry powder
  (optional)
½ cup water
2 tablespoons flour
½ cup light cream

Heat pressure cooker. Add oil; brown ham. Stir in peas, curry powder, and water. Close cover securely. Place pressure regulator on vent pipe. COOK 1 MINUTE. Cool pressure cooker at once. Dissolve flour in cream; stir into pea and ham mixture. Heat, stirring constantly, until thickened. 4 servings.

Molasses is the secret sauce ingredient.

PORK CHOW MEIN

1½ lbs. lean pork shoulder,
  cut into narrow
  3 to 4-inch strips
1 tablespoon shortening
2 teaspoons salt
1 green pepper, cut
  into strips
2 cups diagonally
  sliced celery
1 large onion, sliced

1 4-ounce can pimientos,
  diced
1 4-ounce can mushrooms
1 1-lb. can bean sprouts
2 tablespoons soy sauce
2 tablespoons bead
  molasses
3 tablespoons cornstarch
½ cup water

Heat pressure cooker. Melt shortening; brown meat. Add salt, green pepper, celery, onion, pimientos, and mushrooms. Combine liquid drained from mushrooms and bean sprouts; add soy sauce and molasses. Stir into vegetable combination. Close cover securely. Place pressure regulator on vent pipe. COOK 10 MINUTES. Cool pressure cooker at once. Add bean sprouts, mixing gently. Add combined cornstarch and water to liquid in pressure cooker. Heat, stirring constantly, until gravy has thickened. Serve over chow mein noodles or fluffy rice, if desired. 4 to 6 servings.

Variation: Substitute 3 cups diced cooked roast pork for pork shoulder. COOK 4 MINUTES.

SAUSAGE DINNER-IN-A-DISH

1 lb. pork sausage links
2 onions, diced
5 potatoes, sliced thin
1 16-ounce can cream
  style corn

1½ teaspoons salt
¼ teaspoon pepper
¾ cup tomato juice

Heat pressure cooker. Brown pork links. Remove links from pressure cooker; pour off excess drippings.
In pressure cooker, layer potatoes, onion, and corn. Season with salt and pepper. Place pork links on top; pour tomato juice over all. Close cover securely. Place pressure regulator on vent pipe. COOK 10 MINUTES. Cool pressure cooker at once. Serve garnished with tomato slices or green pepper rings, if desired.
4 to 6 servings.

PORK DINNER

2 lbs. ground pork
  sausage
1½ lbs. potatoes, cut
  into ⅛-inch slices
1 onion, diced

1 9-ounce package
  frozen corn
1½ teaspoons salt
¼ teaspoon pepper
½ cup water

Shape pork sausage into six patties. Heat pressure cooker. Brown patties; remove from pressure cooker. Pour off excess drippings. Layer potatoes, onion, and corn in pressure cooker. Season with salt and pepper. Place patties on top; add water. Close cover securely. Place pressure regulator on vent pipe. COOK 3 MINUTES. Cool pressure cooker at once.
6 servings.

STRICTLY THRIFTY
Sausage Dinner-in-a-Dish or Pork Dinner
Carrot Cole Slaw
Chewy Cherry Dessert (page 202)

For a man-pleasing meal.

SPARERIBS WITH RICE

2½ lbs. spareribs, cut into serving size pieces
1 tablespoon olive oil
1 teaspoon salt
Freshly ground pepper
1 tablespoon brown sugar
1½ cups Burgundy wine
1 cup crushed pineapple and juice
1 tablespoon soy sauce
1 cup brown rice

Heat pressure cooker. Add olive oil; brown spareribs. Remove meat. Combine remaining ingredients in pressure cooker. Replace spareribs. Close cover securely. Place pressure regulator on vent pipe. COOK 15 MINUTES. Let pressure drop of its own accord. 3 to 4 servings.

BARBECUED LIMA BEANS

2 cups dried lima beans
¼ cup cooking oil
1 tablespoon salt
Water

. . . . .

2 slices bacon, diced
¼ cup chopped celery
¼ cup chopped green pepper
¼ cup chopped onion
1 clove garlic, minced
¼ cup chili sauce
⅛ teaspoon mace
⅛ teaspoon basil
1 tablespoon Worcestershire sauce
5 wieners, cut into 1-inch chunks
2 cups tomato juice

Wash dried beans; soak overnight in cooking oil, salt, and enough water to cover completely. Drain; discard liquid. Fry bacon in pressure cooker. Pour off excess dripping. Sauté celery, green pepper, onion, and garlic. Stir in lima beans and remaining ingredients. Close cover securely. Place pressure regulator on vent pipe. COOK 25 MINUTES. Let pressure drop of its own accord. 6 to 8 servings.

For vegetarian fare, omit bacon and wieners.

Halibut and crab team up, skewered with carrots and green pepper. These unusual kabobs are herb-flavored and quick-cooked with rice.

SEAFOOD KEBAB

1 lb. halibut, cut into cubes
½ lb. king crab, cut into 1-inch cubes
1 green pepper, cut into 1-inch squares
1 8-ounce can tiny whole carrots
½ cup cooking oil
¼ cup lemon juice
1 teaspoon salt
¼ teaspoon thyme
¼ teaspoon rosemary
¼ teaspoon tarragon
1 cup rice
¼ cup melted butter
2 cups water

Alternate pieces of halibut, crab, green pepper, and carrot on short skewers. Marinate kebabs in a mixture of oil, lemon juice, salt, thyme, rosemary, and tarragon for 1 hour. Combine rice, melted butter, and water in pressure cooker. Drain kebabs and place in pressure cooker. Close cover securely. Place pressure regulator on vent pipe. COOK 0 MINUTES. Let pressure drop of its own accord. 4 servings.

SHRIMP AND RICE

3 tablespoons cooking oil
½ cup chopped onion
1 cup rice
1 cup beer
¼ cup water
1 teaspoon salt
¼ teaspoon pepper
2 tablespoons lemon juice
1 bay leaf
¾ cup chopped green pepper
1 8-ounce can sliced mushrooms, drained
1½ lbs. frozen shrimp, peeled and cleaned
2 pimientos, sliced

Heat pressure cooker. Add oil; sauté onion and rice. Stir in beer, water, salt, pepper, lemon juice, bay leaf, green pepper, and mushrooms. Add shrimp. Close cover securely. Place pressure regulator on vent pipe. COOK 5 MINUTES. Cool pressure cooker at once. Stir in pimiento. Let stand 5 minutes before serving. 4 to 6 servings.

Just the thing for a ladies' luncheon.
Serve it with tomato bouillon, hot
rolls and a lemony dessert.

HOT TUNA SALAD

1 6½-ounce can tuna,
    drained
1 cup diced celery
½ cup mayonnaise
¼ cup slivered almonds
8 pitted ripe olives, sliced
2 teaspoons lemon juice

1 teaspoon minced onion
2 tablespoons fine dry
    bread crumbs
1 tablespoon grated
    cheese
1 tablespoon butter
½ cup water

Combine tuna, celery, mayonnaise, almonds, olives, lemon
juice, and onion. Spoon into custard cups. Sprinkle
combined bread crumbs and cheese on top. Dot with butter.
Cover with aluminum foil. Place water, cooking rack, and
custard cups in pressure cooker. Close cover securely.
Place pressure regulator on vent pipe. COOK 5 MINUTES.
Cool pressure cooker at once. Garnish with sliced
ripe olives, if desired. 4 to 6 servings.

Variation: Use 1 cup diced cooked chicken in
place of tuna.

An emergency-shelf special.

TUNA PILAF

2 tablespoons cooking oil
1 4-ounce can sliced
    mushrooms, drained
¼ cup chopped onion
¼ cup chopped celery
2 tablespoons chopped
    green pepper
1 cup rice

2 cups water
1 6½-ounce can tuna,
    drained
1 teaspoon Worcestershire
    sauce
½ teaspoon salt
⅛ teaspoon thyme

Heat pressure cooker. Add oil; sauté mushrooms, onion,
celery, and green pepper. Stir in remaining ingredients.
Close cover securely. Place pressure regulator on
vent pipe. COOK 0 MINUTES. Let pressure drop of
its own accord. 4 to 6 servings.

POTATO-TUNA MOLD WITH GOLDEN SAUCE

2½ cups mashed potatoes
3 tablespoons butter
½ cup fine dry bread
   crumbs
1 egg, beaten
1 7-ounce can flaked tuna
1 cup cooked peas
2 tablespoons pickle
   relish

2 cups water
1 1¼-ounce envelope
   chicken gravy mix
1 cup water
¼ cup mayonnaise
2 teaspoons prepared
   yellow mustard
1 teaspoon lemon juice

Combine potatoes, butter, bread crumbs, egg, tuna, peas, and pickle relish. Spoon mixture into buttered mold. Do not fill over ⅔ full. Cover with aluminum foil. Place water, cooking rack, and mold in pressure cooker. Close cover securely. COOK 10 MINUTES. Cool pressure cooker at once. Unmold onto serving platter. Combine chicken gravy mix and water. Heat to boiling, stirring constantly. Add remaining ingredients; heat through. Pour hot sauce over Potato-Tuna Mold. 4 to 6 servings.

CREAMED TUNA-BROCCOLI

1½ lbs. broccoli, cut
   into 1-inch pieces
2 tablespoons lemon juice
¼ teaspoon dill seed

2 6½-ounce cans tuna,
   drained
2 tablespoons water
1 cup thin white sauce

Combine broccoli, lemon juice, dill seed, tuna, and water in pressure cooker. Close cover securely. Place pressure regulator on vent pipe. COOK 2 MINUTES. Cool pressure cooker at once. Stir in white sauce. Serve in hot patty shells, if desired. 4 to 6 servings.

Thin White Sauce: Melt 1 tablespoon butter or margarine. Stir in 1 tablespoon flour and ¼ teaspoon salt. Gradually stir in 1 cup milk and cook, stirring until mixture boils and thickens slightly.

Turkey is not only a best buy in protein but very low in cholesterol.

TANGY TURKEY

3 lbs. turkey, cut into serving pieces
2 tablespoons cooking oil
2 onions, chopped
2 tomatoes, peeled and quartered
1½ teaspoons salt
½ teaspoon pepper
1 clove garlic, minced
1 teaspoon cayenne pepper
1 teaspoon turmeric powder
½ cup water

Heat pressure cooker. Add oil; brown turkey. Sauté onions. Add remaining ingredients. Close cover securely. Place pressure regulator on vent pipe. COOK 10 MINUTES. Cool pressure cooker at once. Thicken gravy, if desired. 4 to 6 servings.

LEMON TURKEY

2 tablespoons butter
2 tablespoons chopped onion
¼ cup chopped celery
1 cup rice
½ teaspoon salt
2 cups cubed cooked turkey
½ cup cooking sherry
1½ cups water
2 tablespoons lemon juice
1 10½-ounce can condensed cream of chicken soup
3 lemon slices

Heat pressure cooker. Add butter; sauté onion and celery. Stir in rice, salt, turkey, sherry, water, and lemon juice. Close cover securely. Place pressure regulator on vent pipe. COOK 0 MINUTES. Let pressure drop of its own accord. Add chicken soup; mix gently. Place in an 11 x 7-inch baking pan; garnish with lemon slices. Brown under the broiler. 4 to 6 servings.

HARVEST TURKEY

2 tablespoons cooking oil
1 cup diced onion
1 cup diced green pepper
2 cups diced cooked turkey
1 cup rice
2 cups apple juice

2 tomatoes, peeled and diced
1 teaspoon salt
¼ teaspoon pepper
1 tablespoon chopped parsley
⅓ cup raisins (optional)

Heat pressure cooker. Add oil; sauté onion and green pepper. Stir in remaining ingredients. Close cover securely. Place pressure regulator on vent pipe. COOK 0 MINUTES. Let pressure drop of its own accord. 4 to 6 servings.

DINNER FOR TWO IN THE COOKER

A chapter within a chapter — dinners for two — prepared all at once in your pressure cooker. Arranging the foods in the pressure cooker as directed is important. But more important: Never fill pressure cooker over ⅔ full. To prepare dinner for one, simply use half the amounts suggested.

DINNER ON THE DOUBLE
Cube Steak
Browned Potatoes
Assorted Vegetables
Pear Halves

Try these handy quick-cooking steaks crusted with corn flakes.

CUBE STEAK

2 cube steaks	1 egg, well beaten
Salt and pepper	1 tablespoon milk
¼ cup corn flake crumbs	2 tablespoons shortening

Season steaks with salt and pepper. Roll in corn flake crumbs, egg, and milk mixture and again in crumbs.

VEGETABLES

Peel potato; cut into slices about 1 inch thick. Season. Peel carrots; slice lengthwise in quarters. Wash green beans and brussel sprouts. Peel yellow turnips. Cut into 1 inch cubes.

Combining Meal

Heat pressure cooker. Add 2 tablespoons shortening; brown steaks on both sides. Lightly brown potato slices. Place cooking rack over steak and potatoes. Arrange vegetables on rack. Add ½ cup water. Close cover securely. Place pressure regulator on vent pipe. COOK 3 MINUTES. Cool pressure cooker at once. Arrange food on serving plates. Thicken gravy, if desired.

Serve two fresh pear halves for dessert with a sprinkling of brown sugar and ginger, if desired.

All AMERICAN FAVORITE
Chicken à la Selecté
Broccoli
Corn on the Cob
Stuffed Pear with Maple Syrup

You can enjoy chicken every Sunday (or any day of the week) teamed with these colorful vegetables.

CHICKEN À LA SELECTÉ

2 pieces chicken, (drum-   Flour and paprika
  stick, thigh, or breast)   2 tablespoons cooking oil
Salt and pepper

Season chicken with salt and pepper. Combine paprika and flour; dredge chicken lightly.

VEGETABLES

Wash broccoli, remove tough section of stem; score ends. Remove husks and silk from corn on the cob.

STUFFED PEARS WITH MAPLE SYRUP

2 pears   2 walnuts, chopped
3 dates, chopped   2 tablespoons maple syrup
2 tablespoons coconut

Wash pears; cut in half lengthwise. Remove core, strings, and stems. Slightly hollow natural indentation. Combine dates, coconut, and walnuts; lightly pack into hollow and stem of pear. Place stuffed pear on a square of aluminum foil. Pinch corners of aluminum foil together over pears.

Combining Meal

Heat pressure cooker. Add 2 tablespoons oil; brown chicken to crispy brown on all sides. Place cooking rack over chicken. Arrange vegetables and fruit on rack. Add ½ cup water. Close cover securely. Place pressure regulator on vent pipe. COOK 5 MINUTES. Cool pressure cooker at once. After removing pears from aluminum foil, pour 1 tablespoon syrup over each pear.

DINNER IN NEXT TO NO TIME
Veal Steaks with Apricots
Sweet Potatoes   Whole Onions
Date Coconut Custard

Fruits make colorful and
nutritious accompaniments
for pressure-cooked meats.

VEAL STEAK WITH APRICOTS

2 veal steaks, ½-inch thick   **2 tablespoons shortening**
Flour   **4 apricots**
Salt and pepper

Lightly dredge veal steaks in flour; sprinkle with salt and pepper. Wash apricots, set aside until time to place in pressure cooker.

VEGETABLES

Wash sweet potato; cut in half lengthwise. Peel onions.

DATE COCONUT CUSTARD

1 egg, well beaten   **4 dates, chopped**
1 tablespoon sugar   **1 tablespoon shredded**
⅛ teaspoon salt   **coconut**
½ teaspoon vanilla   **⅛ teaspoon nutmeg**
¾ cup milk

Combine egg, sugar, salt, and vanilla. Add milk; mix well. Divide chopped dates and coconut equally into 2 custard cups. Pour custard mixture into each cup. Sprinkle nutmeg on top. Cover with aluminum foil.

Combining Meal

Heat pressure cooker. Add 2 tablespoons shortening; brown meat to crispy brown on both sides. Arrange apricots around meat. Place cooking rack over meat and apricots. Set custard cups and vegetables on rack. Add ½ cup water. Close cover securely. Place pressure regulator on vent pipe. COOK 5 MINUTES. Cool pressure cooker at once. When serving, lift skins from potatoes. If desired, spoon one tablespoon of maple syrup or honey over top of potatoes.

SO GOOD AND SO GOOD FOR YOU
Liver and Bacon
Potato Slices
Assorted Vegetables
'Baked' Apple

Liver and bacon go together
like love and marriage.

LIVER AND BACON

2 slices bacon   **1 slice onion,**
½ lb. beef liver   **sectioned into rings**

Fry bacon in pressure cooker. Remove bacon; drain on paper towel. Brown liver and onion rings.

VEGETABLES

Peel potato; cut into slices about ¾ of an inch thick. Wash lima beans and broccoli. Remove tough section of broccoli stem; score ends. Peel carrots; slice lengthwise into quarters. Season vegetables, if desired.

'BAKED' APPLE

Wash and core two apples. Sugar may be added before or after cooking. Place apples on a square of aluminum foil. Pinch corners of aluminum foil together over apple.

Combining Meal

Place cooking rack over liver, onion rings, and potato slices in pressure cooker. Arrange vegetables and foil wrapped apples on rack. Add ½ cup water. Close cover securely. Place pressure regulator on vent pipe. COOK 3 MINUTES. Cool pressure cooker at once. Garnish each serving with a slice of bacon.

SUPPER SWEDISH-AMERICAN STYLE
Swedish Meat Balls
Thick-sliced Potatoes
Corn and Lima Beans
Vanilla Custard

Every ethnic group has its special way of seasoning meatballs; the nutmeg and ginger are the secret in these.

SWEDISH MEATBALLS

¼ lb. ground beef
¼ lb. ground pork
1 egg
2 teaspoons flour
1 small onion, grated
1 clove garlic, grated
Salt, pepper, and paprika

Dash of nutmeg
Dash of ginger
2 tablespoons parsley, finely cut
Enough milk to combine
2 tablespoons butter

Combine all ingredients, except butter; mold into six meatballs.

VEGETABLES

Peel potato, cut into slices about ¾ of an inch thick. Season corn and lima beans with salt, pepper, and butter; wrap in aluminum foil.

VANILLA CUSTARD

Follow directions for Date Custard, page 160; omit dates and coconut, and increase sugar to 3 tablespoons.

Combining Meal

Heat pressure cooker. Add 2 tablespoons butter; brown meat balls and potato slices. Place cooking rack over meat balls and potatoes. Arrange vegetables and custard cups on rack. Add ½ cup water. Close cover securely. Place pressure regulator on vent pipe. COOK 3 MINUTES. Cool pressure cooker at once. Chill custards until ready to serve.

EXCELLENCE WITH EASE
Pork Chops with Glazed Prunes
Browned Potatoes and Carrots
Cauliflower with Cheese
Valentine Apples

Pork is always delicious when
prepared in the pressure cooker.

PORK CHOPS WITH GLAZED PRUNES

2 pork chops,
½-inch thick
Salt and pepper
¼ cup corn flake crumbs

1 egg, well beaten
1 tablespoon milk
2 tablespoons shortening
4 dried prunes

Season pork chops with salt and pepper. Roll in corn flake crumbs, then in egg and milk mixture, and again in crumbs. Wash prunes in warm water; soak in water until time to place in pressure cooker.

VEGETABLES

Peel potatoes; slice into quarters lengthwise. Peel carrots; slice in half lengthwise. Break cauliflower into flowerettes; wash in salted water. Score stem ends.

VALENTINE APPLES

Follow directions for "Baked" Apples, page 161, except fill apples with mixture of 4 chopped dates and 2 tablespoons chopped walnuts.

Combining Meal

Heat pressure cooker. Add 2 tablespoons shortening; brown meat on both sides to crispy brown. Slightly brown potatoes and carrots. Place cooking rack over meat, potatoes, and carrots. Arrange apples, prunes, and cauliflower on rack. Add ½ cup of water. Close cover securely. Place pressure regulator on vent pipe. COOK 5 MINUTES. Cool pressure cooker at once. Unwrap apples. If desired, pour honey over apples at once to produce glazed appearance. Sprinkle grated Parmesan cheese over cauliflower before serving.

VEGETABLES AND RICE

*Are you the cook for a house full of vegetable haters?
Or perhaps they balk when you serve asparagus or
zucchini in place of the expected peas, beans, or corn?
You and your pressure cooker can do a lot to change
their minds if you give vegetables special attention.*

*First, pressure-cooked vegetables retain their vivid
colors, delicious flavor, and health-giving vitamins and
minerals. Second, the time you save with the pressure
cooker can be used for special combinations, seasonings,
and garnishes to present the vegetables attractively.*

*Whether your vegetables are from garden or market,
frozen, canned or dried, here is a wealth of ideas to
convert your family to vegetable eaters, if not
vegetable lovers.*

*This chapter also includes a collection of rice
dishes, imaginative treatments of the little grain that
has sustained the world's population for centuries.*

*April, May and June are
asparagus months. Choose
spears that are round, smooth,
deep green, and firm. The
tips on top quality asparagus
are still tightly closed.*

APRIL ASPARAGUS SALAD

2 lbs. asparagus spears   ⅓ cup red wine
2 green onions, chopped   ¾ cup Italian salad
6 stuffed olives, sliced   dressing

Wash and trim asparagus; place in pressure cooker.
Combine remaining ingredients; pour over asparagus.
Close cover securely. Place pressure regulator on
vent pipe. COOK 3 MINUTES. Cool pressure cooker
at once. Chill. Drain; serve on a bed of lettuce or
other greens. 4 servings.

*This is excellent as an
accompaniment for veal or
chicken. Or serve it as a ladies'
luncheon dish with cheese rolls.*

SPRING ASPARAGUS

2 lbs. asparagus   ½ teaspoon thyme
2 green onions, chopped   ⅓ cup red wine
6 stuffed olives, chopped   ¼ cup wine vinegar
1 tablespoon capers   ¾ cup olive oil
1 teaspoon salt   ½ teaspoon pepper

Wash and trim asparagus; place in pressure cooker.
Combine remaining ingredients; pour over asparagus.
Close cover securely. Place pressure regulator on
vent pipe. COOK 3 MINUTES. Cool pressure cooker
at once. Drain. 4 servings.

ASPARAGUS 'N SAUCE

1 10-ounce package
frozen asparagus spears
¼ cup hot water

1 teaspoon instant
bouillon
1 tablespoon soy sauce

Place asparagus in pressure cooker. Combine remaining ingredients; pour over asparagus. Close cover securely. Place pressure regulator on vent pipe. COOK 3 MINUTES. Cool pressure cooker at once. Thicken sauce, if desired. 2 to 3 servings.

*Here's the popular green bean
in cream soup casserole
adapted for the pressure
cooker. Remember this when
it's too hot to use the oven.*

ORIENTAL GREEN BEANS

1 10-ounce package
frozen green beans
½ cup bean sprouts
½ cup sliced mushrooms
¾ teaspoon salt

½ 10½-ounce can
condensed cream of
mushroom soup
¼ cup sliced almonds,
toasted
1 cup water

Combine green beans, sprouts, mushrooms, salt, soup, and 2 tablespoons almonds. Place in bowl which will fit loosely in pressure cooker. Do not fill bowl over ⅔ full. Place water, cooking rack, and bowl in pressure cooker. Close cover securely. Place pressure regulator on vent pipe. COOK 10 MINUTES.
Cool pressure cooker at once. Sprinkle remaining almonds on vegetables. 4 servings.

*They're high in
vegetable protein.*

BUTTER BEANS

2 cups dried butter beans
  or baby lima beans
¼ cup cooking oil
1 tablespoon salt
  Water
· · · · · ·

¾ cup melted butter
¾ cup brown sugar
1 tablespoon dry mustard
1 tablespoon molasses
  Water
1 cup sour cream

Wash dried butter beans; soak overnight in cooking
oil, salt, and enough water to cover completely. Drain;
discard liquid. Combine butter beans, butter,
brown sugar, dry mustard, and molasses in pressure
cooker. Stir in enough water to well cover beans.
Close cover securely. Place pressure regulator on
vent pipe. COOK 25 MINUTES. Let pressure drop of its
own accord. Stir in sour cream; heat through.
8 servings.

*A zippy vegetable to
complement any roast meat.
This method of vegetable
cookery — braising in bouillon
— is employed by chefs
the world over.*

GREEN BEANS IN MUSTARD AND WINE

2 tablespoons butter
1 teaspoon instant beef
  bouillon
½ teaspoon dry mustard
¼ cup water

2 tablespoons dry white
  wine
1 lb. green beans, cut
  into 1-inch pieces
¼ cup slivered almonds,
  toasted

Heat pressure cooker; melt butter. Add remaining
ingredients except almonds. Close cover securely.
Place pressure regulator on vent pipe. COOK 3
MINUTES. Cool pressure cooker at once. Stir in
almonds. 4 servings.

The texture and mild flavor of beans make them an excellent foil for herbs. Basil is also delicious with tomatoes, while rosemary goes well with peas.

GREEN BEANS WITH HERB SAUCE

1 lb. green beans	¼ teaspoon dried basil
1 onion, sliced	¾ teaspoon salt
1 clove garlic, minced	2 tablespoons parsley
¼ cup chopped celery	¼ cup wine vinegar
1 tablespoon sesame seed	¼ cup water
¼ teaspoon rosemary	1 tablespoon butter

Wash and trim beans; cut crosswise into thin slanted slices. Combine remaining ingredients; pour over beans in pressure cooker. Close cover securely. Place pressure regulator on vent pipe. COOK 3 MINUTES. Cool pressure cooker at once. 4 servings.

LIMA BEAN CASSEROLE

2 cups dried lima beans	⅛ teaspoon curry powder
¼ cup cooking oil	1 20-ounce can tomatoes
1 tablespoon salt	1 teaspoon Worcestershire sauce
Water	Water
. . . . .	
1 tablespoon brown sugar	12 ounces dry cottage cheese
¾ cup chopped onion	1 cup walnuts
¼ teaspoon dry mustard	

Wash dried lima beans; soak overnight in cooking oil, salt, and enough water to cover completely. Drain; discard liquid. Combine brown sugar, onion, dry mustard, curry powder, tomatoes, and Worcestershire sauce. Pour over lima beans in pressure cooker. Add enough water to well cover beans. Close cover securely. Place pressure regulator on vent pipe. COOK 25 MINUTES. Let pressure drop of its own accord. Fold in cottage cheese and nuts. Serve immediately. 6 to 8 servings.

YELLOW BEANS BERLIN

2 lbs. yellow or
   wax beans
¼ cup chopped green
   onions

2 tablespoons prepared
   mustard
½ teaspoon salt
½ cup chicken broth

Combine all ingredients in pressure cooker. Close
cover securely. Place pressure regulator on vent pipe.
COOK 3 MINUTES. Cool pressure cooker at once.
Thicken sauce, if desired. 6 to 8 servings.

*Vegetable Plate Supper: For a change of pace, serve a plate of
three vegetables: yellow like Beans Berlin, green like Alpine
Broccoli and red, perhaps broiled tomato halves. Center plate
with seasoned cottage cheese.*

ALPINE BROCCOLI

2 10-ounce packages
   frozen broccoli spears

1 10½-ounce can
   condensed chicken
   rice soup
4 slices Swiss cheese

Place broccoli and soup in pressure cooker. Close
cover securely. Place pressure regulator on vent pipe.
COOK 2 MINUTES. Cool pressure cooker at once.
Place broccoli in a baking dish. Top with Swiss cheese
slices. Broil until cheese is bubbly. 6 servings.

Variation: Substitute 2 lbs. of garden-fresh broccoli
for the frozen broccoli. COOK 3 MINUTES.

*This would be an excellent vegetable
for a dieter — just skip the butter.
Use of the rack prevents the delicate
flowerets from getting water logged.*

BROCCOLI À LA CITRUS

2 lbs. broccoli
½ cup water
1 tablespoon butter

1 grapefruit, sectioned
Salt and pepper

Place water, cooking rack, and broccoli in pressure
cooker. Close cover securely. Place pressure
regulator on vent pipe. COOK 3 MINUTES. Cool
pressure cooker at once. Melt butter; sauté grapefruit
sections. Sprinkle salt and pepper on broccoli.
Arrange grapefruit sections over top. 4 to 6 servings.

*Remember this as a luncheon
dish for another occasion.*

BROCCOLI DOMINGO

1½ lbs. broccoli spears
1 cup diced cooked ham
½ cup sliced stuffed
olives
⅛ teaspoon nutmeg
¼ teaspoon salt

Dash cayenne pepper
½ cup water
2 tablespoons butter
2 tablespoons flour
1 cup light cream

Place first seven ingredients into pressure cooker. Close
cover securely. Place pressure regulator on vent pipe.
COOK 1 MINUTE. Cool pressure cooker at once.
Remove broccoli to platter. Add remaining ingredients;
blend until thickened. Pour sauce over broccoli.
If desired, garnish with grated Swiss cheese;
broil a few seconds. 6 servings.

Smaller sprouts have a more delicate flavor than larger, looser ones.

BRUSSELS SPROUTS WITH CRUNCH

3 lbs. Brussels sprouts
½ cup chicken broth
¼ teaspoon salt
White pepper

¼ teaspoon basil
1 5-ounce can water chestnuts, sliced
2 tablespoons butter

Place Brussels sprouts in pressure cooker. Combine remaining ingredients; pour over sprouts. Close cover securely. Place pressure regulator on vent pipe. COOK 2 MINUTES. Cool pressure cooker at once. 6 to 8 servings.

BRUSSELS SPROUTS WITH NUTMEG

2 10-ounce packages frozen Brussels sprouts
½ cup water
1 teaspoon salt

1 teaspoon ground nutmeg
⅛ teaspoon pepper
2 tablespoons butter

Place Brussels sprouts and water into pressure cooker. Close cover securely. Place pressure regulator on vent pipe. COOK 3 MINUTES. Cool pressure cooker at once. Drain water. Sprinkle seasonings over sprouts. Dot with butter. 6 to 8 servings.

This vegetable can double as salad.

WILTED CABBAGE

6 slices bacon, diced
1 lb. cabbage, shredded
¼ cup vinegar

1 teaspoon salt
2 teaspoons sugar

Fry bacon in pressure cooker. Remove excess drippings. Add remaining ingredients; toss well. Close cover securely. Place pressure regulator on vent pipe. COOK 0 MINUTES. Cool pressure cooker at once. Serve hot. 4 servings.

These delicate little vegetable custards are gourmet fare. They are attractive as a first course, luncheon main dish or accompaniment for roasts or chops. Also called timbales.

CARROT RAMEKIN

2 tablesoons butter
2 tablespoons flour
¾ cup milk
1 teaspoon salt
¼ teaspoon pepper

2 eggs, beaten
2 cups cooked diced carrots
½ cup water

Melt butter; blend in flour. Add milk; heat until thickened. Add salt and pepper. Beat white sauce mixture into eggs. Stir in vegetables. Spoon into buttered custard cups. Cover custard cups with aluminum foil. Place water, cooking rack, and custard cups in pressure cooker. Close cover securely. Place pressure regulator on vent pipe. COOK 3 MINUTES. Cool pressure cooker at once. Unmold. 4 to 6 servings.

Variations:

Beet Ramekin: Substitute cubed beets for carrots and add 1 teaspoon chopped onion.

Corn Ramekin: Substitute whole kernel corn for carrots and add 1 teaspoon chopped onion, 2 tablespoons chopped green pepper, and 1 tablespoon chopped pimiento.

Spinach Ramekin: Substitute chopped cooked spinach for carrots.

Rutabaga Ramekin: Substitute cooked, mashed rutabaga for carrots.

Vegetable Ramekin: Substitute mixed vegetables for carrots.

Cheese Sauce Ramekin: Add 3 tablespoons grated process cheese to the white sauce in any of the above variations.

SOUTHERN CARROTS

2 lbs. carrots, peeled
½ cup water

2 tablespoons dried mint flakes

Place carrots in pressure cooker. Combine water and mint flakes; pour over carrots. Close cover securely. Place pressure regulator on vent pipe. COOK 5 MINUTES. Cool pressure cooker at once. 8 servings.

If your family likes candied sweet potatoes, they will love these glossy carrots.

GLAZED CARROTS

1 lb. carrots, julienne cut
1 cup golden raisins
¼ cup water

4 tablespoons butter, melted
½ cup brown sugar
2 tablespoons lemon juice

Combine all ingredients in pressure cooker. Close cover securely. Place pressure regulator on vent pipe. COOK 3 MINUTES. Cool pressure cooker at once. 4 to 6 servings.

Carrots may be rabbit food but they are a valuable source of Vitamin A, for keen eyes. For a more lemon flavor, add 1 teaspoon grated lemon rind.

LEMONY CARROTS

2 lbs. carrots, sliced ¼ inch thick
½ cup water
1 tablespoon lemon juice

¼ teaspoon nutmeg
1 tablespoon chopped parsley
1 tablespoon butter

Combine all ingredients in pressure cooker. Close cover securely. Place pressure regulator on vent pipe. COOK 3 MINUTES. Cool pressure cooker at once. 8 servings.

Remember this recipe when your friends who are natural foods devotees come for dinner.

HONEY-GLAZED CARROTS

1 lb. carrots	½ cup water
½ teaspoon grated	3 tablespoons butter
orange rind	2 tablespoons honey
¼ teaspoon salt	

Place carrots, orange rind, salt, and water in pressure cooker. Close cover securely. Place pressure regulator on vent pipe. COOK 5 MINUTES. Cool pressure cooker at once. Melt butter; add honey and blend. Pour over carrots. 4 servings.

Prime cauliflower is solid and creamy white in color. Any spotting may be cut away.

CAULIFLOWER À LA CHEESE

1 cauliflower	⅓ cup butter
½ cup water	¼ cup flour
½ lb. fresh mushrooms, sliced or 8-ounce can mushroom stems and pieces, drained	1 cup milk
	1 teaspoon salt
	¼ lb. pimiento cheese
¼ cup diced green pepper	Paprika

Wash cauliflower; hollow out core. Place water, cooking rack, and cauliflower in pressure cooker. Close cover securely. Place pressure regulator on vent pipe. COOK 5 MINUTES. Cool pressure cooker at once. Sauté mushrooms and green peppers in butter. Add flour, milk, and salt; cook until thickened. Add cheese; cook until melted. Pour cheese sauce over cauliflower. Sprinkle with paprika. 4 to 6 servings.

Try a Vegetable Platter for your next buffet party. Use Caulfilower à la Cheese as the center of a lovely platter of vegetables. Surround it with alternate servings of a green and white vegetable, such as buttered spinach and glazed onions.

ITALIAN CAULIFLOWER

1 cauliflower, broken
   into flowerets
3 tablespoons olive oil
1 clove garlic, minced
½ teaspoon salt

½ cup tomato juice
1 teaspoon chopped
   parsley
2 tablespoons grated
   Parmesan cheese

Heat pressure cooker. Add oil; sauté garlic and
cauliflowerets. Add salt and tomato juice. Close cover
securely. Place pressure regulator on vent pipe.
COOK 2 MINUTES. Cool pressure cooker at once.
Sprinkle parsley and cheese over top. 4 to 6 servings.

*Four vegetables are better
than one! Especially when
their flavors blend as
beautifully as these do.*

CAULIFLOWER HARLEQUIN

1½ lbs. cauliflowerets
 1 zucchini, sliced
 2 tomatoes, cut into
   wedges

4 slices onion, separated
½ teaspoon salt
⅛ teaspoon thyme
¼ cup water

Combine all ingredients in pressure cooker. Close
cover securely. Place pressure regulator on vent pipe.
COOK 0 MINUTES. Cool pressure cooker at once.
Garnish with a butter square, if desired. 6 to 8 servings.

FIESTA CAULIFLOWER

1 cauliflower, separated
   into flowerets
¼ pound cooked ham,
   cut into slivers

2 teaspoons parsley
½ cup water
2 cooked egg yolks,
   grated

Combine cauliflower, ham, parsley, and water in pressure
cooker. Close cover securely. Place pressure regulator
on vent pipe. COOK 2 MINUTES. Cool pressure cooker
at once. Garnish with grated egg yolk. Serve on
lettuce leaves, if desired. 4 to 6 servings.

*We Americans love bacon.
So why not use bacon to
tempt a timid eater to try
hot cooked celery?*

CELERY AND BACON DELUXE

3 slices fried bacon,
  crumbled
1 onion, sliced
2 tablespoons chopped
  parsley
1 clove garlic, minced

8 ribs celery
1 teaspoon instant beef
  bouillon
¼ cup water
¼ cup buttered bread
  crumbs

Combine all ingredients, except bread crumbs, in pressure
cooker. Close cover securely. Place pressure regulator
on vent pipe. COOK 2 MINUTES. Cool pressure
cooker at once. Place in serving dish; top with
bread crumbs. 4 servings.

*The best celery is solid
with medium-length, thick
stalks and brittle enough to
snap. Choose blanched Golden
or green Pascal celery.*

COUNTRY STYLE CELERY

1 bunch celery, cut into
  1-inch pieces
1 onion, chopped
2 tablespoons butter
1 teaspoon salt

⅛ teaspoon pepper
½ cup water
1 teaspoon instant
  chicken bouillon
  Minced parsley

Combine all ingredients in pressure cooker. Close
cover securely. Place pressure regulator on vent pipe.
COOK 2 MINUTES. Cool pressure cooker at once.
6 to 8 servings.

*If you have a garden or regular access to fresh vegetables, give
Irish bouquets to your friends. Center the "bouquets" with
a small cauliflower or cabbage, add leaf lettuce, beets or
carrots and onions. Roll it all in paper. As lovely as roses
and as welcome — to those who love vegetables.*

CELERY CREOLE

3 cups celery, cut into
   1 inch pieces
¼ cup chopped onion
¼ cup tomato paste
1 clove garlic, chopped

½ teaspoon salt
1 cup pitted ripe olives
½ teaspoon chili powder
½ cup water
Parmesan cheese

Combine all ingredients, except cheese, in pressure cooker. Close cover securely. Place pressure regulator on vent pipe. COOK 2 MINUTES. Cool pressure cooker at once. Garnish with Parmesan cheese. 4 to 6 servings.

CORN-ON-THE-COB

If fresh ears of corn are used, remove corn husks and silk. Frozen ears of corn must stand at room temperature for at least 1½ hours before cooking.

Place 1 cup water, cooking rack, and ears of corn in pressure cooker. Do not fill over ⅔ full. Close cover securely. Place pressure regulator on vent pipe. COOK FRESH CORN 3 TO 5 MINUTES; FROZEN CORN 2 MINUTES. Cool pressure cooker at once.

You may want to use plain butter on 1 or 2 ears for the children.

HERBED CORN-ON-THE-COB

½ cup melted butter
½ teaspoon rosemary
¼ teaspoon marjoram
½ teaspoon salt

¼ teaspoon pepper
¼ teaspoon parsley
5 ears sweet corn
½ cup water

Combine melted butter, rosemary, marjoram, salt, pepper, and parsley. Brush corn with butter mixture. Wrap each ear of sweet corn with aluminum foil. Place water, cooking rack, and corn in pressure cooker. Close cover securely. Place pressure regulator on vent pipe. COOK 5 MINUTES. Cool pressure cooker at once. 5 servings.

*An ideal way to use leftover
corn-on-the-cob. Also delicious
with canned corn.*

CORN SCALLOP

2 **cups whole kernel corn**
¼ **cup cream**
2 **eggs, beaten**
½ **teaspoon grated onion**
¼ **teaspoon salt**
⅛ **teaspoon pepper**

½ **cup soda cracker
crumbs**
1 **cup shredded cheddar
cheese**
½ **cup water**

Combine all ingredients, except water and ¼ cup
cheese. Spoon corn mixture into custard cups. Top
with remaining cheese. Cover with aluminum foil.
Place water, cooking rack, and custard cups in pressure
cooker. Close cover securely. Place pressure regulator
on vent pipe. COOK 3 MINUTES. Cool pressure
cooker at once. 6 servings.

*If you have never eaten cooked
cucumber, you and your family
have a new flavor and texture
sensation in store for you.*

CUCUMBERS 'N WINE

2 **large cucumbers,
peeled**
1 **onion, sliced**

½ **teaspoon basil**
¼ **cup dry white wine**
¼ **cup water**

Slice cucumbers lengthwise. Separate onion slices
into rings. Place all ingredients in pressure cooker.
Close cover securely. Place pressure regulator on
vent pipe. COOK 3 MINUTES. Cool pressure cooker
at once. 4 servings.

*French dressing provides a
seasoning shortcut since it's
oil, vinegar and seasonings
all in one. Remember it, too,
for marinating meats.*

FRENCH EGGPLANT

2 lbs. eggplant, cut into
1-inch slices
¾ cup French dressing

¼ cup water
½ cup sour cream

Peel eggplant slices. Place eggplant, French dressing,
and water in pressure cooker. Close cover securely.
Place pressure regulator on vent pipe. COOK 2 MINUTES.
Cool pressure cooker at once. Drain. Garnish with
sour cream. 6 servings.

*Okra is also good with . . .
chili powder, garlic, mustard,
oregano, and bacon.*

OKRA PIQUANT

2 tablespoons butter
½ cup chopped green
onion
2 lbs. okra, cut into
½-inch pieces

2 tablespoons lemon
juice
2 tablespoons water

Heat pressure cooker. Melt butter; sauté onion.
Add okra, lemon juice, and water. Stir gently. Close
cover securely. Place pressure regulator on vent pipe.
COOK 3 MINUTES. Cool pressure cooker at once.
6 to 8 servings.

PEANUTTY ONIONS

12 small onions, peeled
 2 tablespoons butter
¼ cup water

¾ cup salted Virginia
  peanuts
 2 tablespoons brown sugar

Combine all ingredients in pressure cooker. Close
cover securely. Place pressure regulator on vent pipe.
COOK 5 MINUTES. Cool pressure cooker at once.
3 to 4 servings.

ONIONS 'N ALMOND SAUCE

16 small onions, peeled
½ cup hot water
 1 tablespoon instant
   chicken bouillon

¼ teaspoon almond
  extract
½ teaspoon salt

Combine all ingredients in pressure cooker. Close
cover securely. Place pressure regulator on vent pipe.
COOK 5 MINUTES. Cool pressure cooker at once.
If desired, top with slivered almonds. 4 servings.

*Weight-conscious families are now serving a green vegetable
with a yellow vegetable like squash or a white vegetable
like onions in place of potatoes, noodles, or rice.*

This often-ignored vegetable can add welcome variety to winter vegetable choices. The best parsnips are smooth, firm, well-shaped, and small to medium size.

PARSNIPS WITH ROSEMARY

¼ cup butter
2 lbs. parsnips, peeled and cut into ½-inch slices
½ teaspoon dried rosemary, crushed

½ cup water
½ cup Parmesan cheese

Heat pressure cooker. Melt butter; stir in parsnips, rosemary, and water. Close cover securely. Place pressure regulator on vent pipe. COOK 3 MINUTES. Cool pressure cooker at once. Garnish parsnips with Parmesan cheese. 4 to 6 servings.

The sweet 'snip becomes even sweeter with the addition of naturally sweet orange juice. Perfect with pork.

PARSNIPS IN ORANGE SAUCE

2 lbs. parsnips, peeled and cut lengthwise
½ cup fresh orange juice

2 tablespoons sugar
½ teaspoon salt
4 orange slices

Place parsnips in pressure cooker. Combine orange juice, sugar, and salt; pour over parsnips. Add orange slices. Close cover securely. Place pressure regulator on vent pipe. COOK 5 MINUTES. Cool pressure cooker at once. 4 to 6 servings.

Parsnips in butterscotch sauce.

GLAZED PARSNIPS

1 lb. parsnips cut into
¼-inch slices
¼ cup butter, melted
1 tablespoon honey

¼ cup brown sugar
2 tablespoons chopped
almonds, toasted
⅓ cup water

Place parsnips in pressure cooker. Combine remaining
ingredients; pour over parsnips. Close cover securely.
Place pressure regulator on vent pipe. COOK 4 MINUTES.
Cool pressure cooker at once. 3 to 4 servings.

Enjoy June — have fresh peas.

PEAS 'N BACON

½ lb. bacon, diced
2 lbs. peas
½ teaspoon sugar

2 cups sliced green onion
½ cup water

Fry bacon in pressure cooker. Pour off excess drippings.
Add remaining ingredients. Close cover securely.
Place pressure regulator on vent pipe. COOK 2
MINUTES. Cool pressure cooker at once. Thicken
sauce, if desired. 4 to 6 servings.

PEAS ALMONDINE

3 tablespoons butter
½ cup slivered blanched
almonds
2 10-ounce packages
frozen peas or 1½
pounds fresh peas,
shelled

2 teaspoons instant
chopped onion
½ teaspoon salt
½ cup water

Heat pressure cooker. Melt butter; sauté almonds.
Remove; set aside. Place remaining ingredients in
pressure cooker. Close cover securely. Place pressure
regulator on vent pipe. COOK 1 MINUTE. Cool
pressure cooker at once. Garnish with browned almonds.
6 to 8 servings.

*Use of the pressure cooker
makes it unnecessary to
parboil the peppers*

CURRY STUFFED PEPPERS

½ lb. pork sausage	¼ cup chopped onion
½ cup cooked rice	Salt and pepper
½ cup whole kernel corn	4 green peppers, cored
¼ teaspoon curry powder	1 cup water

Brown pork sausage. Combine sausage, rice, corn, curry powder, onion, salt, and pepper. Stuff the green peppers. Place water, cooking rack, and peppers in pressure cooker. Close cover securely. Place pressure regulator on vent pipe. COOK 3 MINUTES. Cool pressure cooker at once. 4 servings.

*From sunny Italy, an elegant
stuffed pepper to grace your
party table.*

POZZUOLI PEPPERS

4 green peppers	2 tablespoons capers
½ cup chopped onions	¼ cup sliced black olives
2 3-ounce cans sliced mushrooms	⅛ teaspoon oregano
1 tablespoon olive oil	2 tablespoons tomato paste
1½ cups bread crumbs	1 cup water
4 anchovies, shredded	

Cut a one-inch piece from the stem end of the peppers; scoop out the seeds and fibers. Sauté onions and mushrooms in oil. Stir in bread crumbs, anchovies, capers, olives, oregano, and tomato paste. Stuff the peppers. Place water, cooking rack, and peppers in pressure cooker. Close cover securely. Place pressure regulator on vent pipe. COOK 5 MINUTES. Cool pressure cooker at once. 4 servings.

Variation: Substitute ¼ cup crumbled fried bacon for the anchovies and capers.

*A dish to do you proud at
your next company dinner.*

ELEGANTE POTATOES

1½ lbs. potatoes, peeled
    and cut into ½-inch
    cubes
  1 clove garlic, minced
  ¼ cup sliced green onion
  ¾ teaspoon salt

½ cup water
 . . . . .
½ cup sour cream
½ cup cottage cheese
½ cup fine bread
    crumbs, buttered

Gently mix potatoes, garlic, onion, and salt in pressure
cooker. Add water. Close cover securely. Place
pressure regulator on vent pipe. COOK 3 MINUTES.
Cool pressure cooker at once. Drain potatoes.
Combine sour cream and cottage cheese; add to potatoes
and heat through. Pour potato mixture into serving bowl.
Top with buttered crumbs. 6 servings.

GARDEN-FRESH POTATOES

2 lbs. new red potatoes
¼ cup parsley

½ cup water
¼ cup melted butter

Remove a strip of peel from around the center of each
potato. Place potatoes, parsley, and water in pressure
cooker. Close cover securely. Place pressure regulator
on vent pipe. COOK 4 MINUTES. Cool pressure
cooker at once. Place potatoes in serving bowl;
garnish with melted butter. 6 to 8 servings.

POTATOES À LA CHEDDAR

6 potatoes, cut into
    ½-inch slices
¼ cup butter
2 tablespoons chopped
    onion

½ cup tomato juice
½ cup grated Cheddar
    cheese

Combine potatoes, butter, onions, and tomato juice in
pressure cooker. Close cover securely. Place pressure
regulator on vent pipe. COOK 2 MINUTES. Cool
pressure cooker at once. Garnish with grated cheese.
6 servings.

The pressure cooker version of the popular twice-baked potatoes.

SOUFFLED POTATOES

3 baking potatoes
1 cup water
¼ cup warm cream
Salt and white pepper

4 tablespoons butter
¾ cup shredded Cheddar cheese
Paprika

Place water, cooking rack, and potatoes in pressure cooker. Close cover securely. Place pressure regulator on vent pipe. COOK 10 MINUTES. Cool pressure cooker at once. Cut potatoes in half lengthwise. Scoop out potato; reserve shells. Mash potato; add cream, salt, pepper, and butter. Whip until fluffy. Lightly pile potato mixture into shells. Top with shredded cheese; broil until cheese is bubbly. Sprinkle with paprika. 6 servings.

Also called yellow turnip, the rutabaga and its smaller cousin, the white turnip, are neglected vegetables in this country. In Europe they are often used in stews and soups.

PARTY RUTABAGA

2 slices bacon, diced
2 lbs. rutabaga, cubed
½ cup chopped onion
1 tablespoon chopped parsley
½ teaspoon salt

⅛ teaspoon cayenne pepper
½ cup water
1 tablespoon flour
2 tablespoons butter

Fry bacon in pressure cooker. Pour off excess drippings. Add rutabaga, onion, parsley, salt, pepper, and water. Close cover securely. Place pressure regulator on vent pipe. COOK 3 MINUTES. Cool pressure cooker at once. Sprinkle flour over rutabaga. Add butter, stirring until sauce is thickened. 4 to 6 servings.

SOYBEANS WITH PEARL ONIONS

2 cups dried soybeans
¼ cup cooking oil
1 tablespoon salt
Water

. . . . .

1 tablespoon peanut oil
2 tablespoons chopped green pepper

16 pearl onions
½ teaspoon salt
⅛ teaspoon pepper
Carrot juice
¼ cup chopped unsalted peanuts

Wash dried soybeans; soak overnight in cooking oil, salt, and enough water to cover completely. Drain; discard liquid. Heat pressure cooker. Add peanut oil; sauté green pepper. Stir in soybeans, onions, salt, and pepper. Add enough carrot juice to well cover beans. Close cover securely. Place pressure regulator on vent pipe. COOK 40 MINUTES. Let pressure drop of its own accord. Garnish with unsalted peanuts. 6 to 8 servings.

The carrot juice in this recipe may be either canned, or liquefied in a blender from fresh carrots.

Popeye's favorite,
dressed up for a party.

FANCY SPINACH

2 slices bacon, diced
¼ cup chopped onion
2 lbs. spinach, chopped

¼ cup water
¼ cup cream

Fry bacon in pressure cooker. Pour off excess drippings. Sauté onion. Add spinach and water. Close cover securely. Place pressure regulator on vent pipe. COOK 1 MINUTE. Cool pressure cooker at once. Add cream and stir gently. 4 to 6 servings.

GLAZED SWEET POTATOES

6 sweet potatoes, peeled
and cut lengthwise
1 cup maple-blended
syrup

2 tablespoons melted
butter
2 teaspoons salt
½ cup water

Place sweet potatoes in pressure cooker. Combine remaining ingredients; pour over potatoes. Close cover securely. Place pressure regulator on vent pipe. COOK 5 MINUTES. Cool pressure cooker at once. 6 servings.

Golden 'n good.

SQUASH CUSTARD

1 cup milk
2 eggs, slightly beaten
3 tablespoons butter, melted
Salt and pepper

2 cups cooked yellow
squash
Bread crumbs
½ cup water

Scald milk; cool slightly. Combine eggs, butter, salt, pepper, and squash. Add milk slowly, stirring constantly. Pour into custard cups. Sprinkle with bread crumbs; cover with aluminum foil. Place water, cooking rack, and custard cups in pressure cooker. Close cover securely. Place pressure regulator on vent pipe. COOK 5 MINUTES. Cool pressure cooker at once. 4 to 6 servings.

HAWAIIAN STUFFED SQUASH

1 buttercup squash cut in
half, seeds removed
1 teaspoon salt
2 tablespoons brown sugar
¼ cup crushed pineapple

2 tablespoons chopped
walnuts
1 teaspoon melted butter
½ cup water

Sprinkle salt on squash. Combine brown sugar, pineapple, walnuts, and butter. Spoon into squash cavities. Place water, cooking rack, and squash in pressure cooker. Close cover securely. COOK 12 MINUTES. Cool pressure cooker at once. 4 servings.

Variation: Substitute acorn squash for buttercup squash. COOK 10 to 12 MINUTES.

This colorful vegetable should be enjoyed often in August and September when fresh, full-flavored tomatoes are plentiful. It is the right meal-mate for any meat.

SCALLOPED TOMATOES

2 cups peeled, cubed
fresh tomatoes
½ cup sour cream
½ teaspoon salt
2 teaspoons sugar
1 tablespoon butter
2 tablespoons diced
green pepper

2 tablespoons sliced
green onion
½ cup whole kernel corn
1 tablespoon flour
1 cup water

Place tomatoes in a bowl which fits loosely in pressure cooker. Combine remaining ingredients, except water; pour over tomatoes. Place water, cooking rack, and bowl in pressure cooker. Close cover securely. Place pressure regulator on vent pipe. COOK 10 MINUTES. Cool pressure cooker at once. 4 to 6 servings.

DILLY STUFFED TOMATOES

4 tomatoes
Salt and pepper
1½ cups dry bread cubes
1 tablespoon chopped
onion

1 tablespoon chopped
chives
½ teaspoon dill seed
¼ cup melted butter
½ cup water

Slice stem end from tomatoes; remove pulp. Sprinkle inside of tomatoes with salt and pepper. Combine bread cubes, onion, chives, dill seed, butter, and tomato pulp. Stuff tomatoes; place each in a custard cup. Place water, cooking rack, and custard cups in pressure cooker. Close cover securely. Place pressure regulator on vent pipe. COOK 3 MINUTES. Cool pressure cooker at once. 4 servings.

Dark green zucchini is also delicious raw, either sliced and added to green salad, or cut in sticks and served with a dip.

ZUCCHINI WHEELS

2 lbs. zucchini squash, cut into ½-inch wheels

½ cup water

1 tablespoon minced onion

¼ teaspoon grated lemon peel

1½ tablespoons lemon juice

2 tablespoons dried parsley flakes

Place squash in pressure cooker. Combine remaining ingredients; pour over squash. Close cover securely. Place pressure regulator on vent pipe. COOK 3 MINUTES. Cool pressure cooker at once. 4 to 6 servings.

ZUCCHINI SALAD

6 zucchini, cut in half lengthwise

½ cup water

½ teaspoon salt

¾ cup chopped radishes

¾ cup chopped cucumber

¼ cup chopped celery

¼ cup Italian salad dressing

Salt and pepper

Place water, cooking rack, and zucchini in pressure cooker. Add salt. Close cover securely. Place pressure regulator on vent pipe. COOK 4 MINUTES. Cool pressure cooker at once. Chill zucchini; hollow out, leaving one-half inch shells. Chop or mash pulp; combine with remaining ingredients. Refill shells. Serve cold on greens, if desired. 6 servings.

Equally good made with moist,
sweet yams, or the drier,
mealy sweet potatoes.

ORANGE CANDIED YAMS

6 yams, peeled and
  halved
1 teaspoon grated
  orange rind

1 cup brown sugar
¼ cup butter
1 teaspoon salt
1½ cups orange juice

Place all ingredients in pressure cooker. Close cover
securely. Place pressure regulator on vent pipe.
COOK 6 MINUTES. Cool pressure cooker at once.
6 servings.

Serving a vegetable main dish every
week or two helps beat the high
cost of eating. Vary this recipe with
flowerets, or sliced mushrooms.

VEGETABLE CHOP SUEY

3 tablespoons butter
1 onion, sliced
3 cups sliced celery
1 green pepper, cut into
  1-inch strips
1 cup cut green beans
1 cup bean sprouts

1 cup sliced water
  chestnuts
1 teaspoon salt
1 tablespoon instant
  vegetable bouillon
1 tablespoon soy sauce
1 cup water

Heat pressure cooker. Add butter; sauté onion. Add
remaining ingredients. Close cover securely. Place
pressure regulator on vent pipe. COOK 3 MINUTES.
Cool pressure cooker at once. Serve on cooked rice
or chow mein noodles, if desired. 6 servings.

*Just for fun, call this
Tomatoed Potatoes.*

VEGETABLE COMBO

1 onion, chopped	2 tomatoes, cut
1 tablespoon cooking oil	into wedges
½ cup water	4 potatoes, diced
2 green peppers, cut	1 teaspoon salt
into strips	½ teaspoon pepper

Heat pressure cooker. Add oil; sauté onion. Add water,
green peppers, tomatoes, potatoes, salt, and pepper.
Close cover securely. Place pressure regulator
on vent pipe. COOK 3 MINUTES. Cool pressure cooker
at once. 6 servings.

*SUPPER ON A HOT SUMMER DAY
Vegetable Combo
or
Mixed Vegetables
Platter of Cold Cuts and Cheeses
Tossed Green Salad
Lemon Sherbet with Chocolate Sauce*

*A hot vegetable with something
for everyone. Feel free to
adapt the mixture to your
personal preference — more
potatoes, less corn, whatever
you have on hand.*

MIXED VEGETABLES

½ cup diced potatoes	½ cup corn
½ cup cut green beans	2 tablespoons butter
½ cup sliced carrots	¼ teaspoon basil
½ cup chopped onions	½ teaspoon salt
½ cup peas	½ cup chicken broth

Combine all ingredients in pressure cooker. Close
cover securely. Place pressure regulator on vent pipe.
COOK 4 MINUTES. Cool pressure cooker at once.
6 servings.

RISOTTO ALLA MARIA

2 cups chicken broth
1 cup rice
1 onion, minced

½ teaspoon saffron
¼ cup butter

Pour chicken broth into pressure cooker; bring to a
boil. Add rice and onion, stirring constantly.
Close cover securely. Place pressure regulator on
vent pipe. COOK 0 MINUTES. Let pressure drop of its
own accord. Add saffron and butter; fluff with a fork.
6 servings.

Browning the rice in oil before
it is cooked gives the rice an
extraordinary eating quality.

FRIED RICE

2 tablespoons cooking oil
1 onion, finely diced
1 cup rice
2 cups water
1 tablespoon soy sauce
½ teaspoon sugar

⅛ teaspoon pepper
1 2-ounce can sliced
   pimientos, drained
2 tablespoons sherry
2 tomatoes, peeled,
   diced and seeded

Heat pressure cooker. Add oil; brown onion and rice.
Add remaining ingredients. Close cover securely. Place
pressure regulator on vent pipe. COOK 0 MINUTES.
Let pressure drop of its own accord. Place in an
11 by 7 inch baking pan; brown under the broiler
5 minutes. 6 servings.

It's smart to be thrifty. Use
liver and other giblets from
your chicken for this easy dish.

LUNCHTIME GIBLETS AND RICE

1 cup rice
1 cup chicken giblets,
   minced
1 teaspoon salt

2 cups chicken broth
2 tablespoons grated
   cheese

Combine first four ingredients in pressure cooker.
Close cover securely. Place pressure regulator on
vent pipe. COOK 0 MINUTES. Let pressure drop of
its own accord. Top with grated cheese.
4 to 6 servings.

MUSHROOM PILAF

1 tablespoon butter
1 cup white rice
½ cup sauterne wine
1½ cups chicken broth
½ teaspoon salt

¼ teaspoon pepper
1 cup sliced mushrooms
1 tablespoon chopped parsley

Combine all ingredients in pressure cooker. Close cover securely. Place pressure regulator on vent pipe. COOK 0 MINUTES. Let pressure drop of its own accord. Lift rice gently with a fork while steaming. 4 to 6 servings.

PEPPERS, TOMATOES 'N RICE

¾ cup water
1 cup beer
2 teaspoons salt
3 tablespoons butter
1 cup rice

4 green peppers, sliced
4 tomatoes, peeled and sliced
1 onion, sliced

Place water, beer, salt, and butter into pressure cooker; bring to boil. Gradually stir in rice. Add green pepper, tomato and onion. Close cover securely. Place pressure regulator on vent pipe. COOK 0 MINUTES. Let pressure drop of its own accord. Lift rice gently with a fork, while steaming. 6 to 8 servings.

PARSLEY RICE RING

1 cup white rice
2 cups water
½ teaspoon salt

2 teaspoons lemon juice
½ cup chopped parsley

Combine all ingredients in pressure cooker. Close
cover securely. Place pressure regulator on vent pipe.
COOK 0 MINUTES. Let pressure drop of its own
accord. Place rice in a buttered ring mold.
While still warm, unmold. 6 servings.

Excellent for a buffet.

RIZ EN CASSEROLE

¼ cup butter
2 onions, chopped
1 green pepper, chopped
2 stalks celery, cut
into diagonal slices
1 cup white rice
1 4-ounce can oysters,
drained

1 teaspoon salt
1 teaspoon poultry
seasoning
½ cup chopped pecans
¼ cup chopped parsley
2 cups chicken bouillon

Heat pressure cooker. Add butter; sauté onions,
green pepper, and celery. Add remaining ingredients;
stir gently. Close cover securely. Place pressure
regulator on vent pipe. COOK 0 MINUTES. Let pressure
drop of its own accord. Lift rice gently with a fork
while steaming. 6 to 8 servings.

TUNA RICE SALAD

1 cup rice
1 6½-ounce can tuna
1 cup shredded carrot
1 cup diced celery
2 tablespoons chopped
    onion
2 cups water

. . . . .
½ cup mayonnaise
2 teaspoons lime juice
¼ teaspoon Worcestershire
    sauce
¼ teaspoon salt
¼ teaspoon salad herbs

Combine first six ingredients in pressure cooker.
Close cover securely. Place pressure regulator on
vent pipe. COOK 0 MINUTES. Let pressure drop of
its own accord. Chill. Blend remaining ingredients
together; toss with rice mixture, before serving.
If desired, serve in a lettuce cup and garnish with
parsley. 6 servings.

HOT GERMAN RICE SALAD

5 slices bacon
1 cup rice
1 cup peas
½ cup chopped celery
¼ cup chopped onion

⅓ cup sugar
3 tablespoons vinegar
½ teaspoon salt
2 cups water

Sauté bacon in pressure cooker. Pour off excess
drippings. Crumble bacon; add remaining ingredients.
Close cover securely. Place pressure regulator on
vent pipe. COOK 0 MINUTES. Let pressure drop of
its own accord. Serve hot. Garnish with bacon curls
and parsley, if desired. 6 to 8 servings.

DESSERTS

What shall we have for dessert? That looked-forward-to sweet to bring a satisfying meal to a close. The rules of smart meal planning read: Consider the complete meal when you plan the dessert. When the meal is light, a filling dessert such as bread pudding will round it out nicely. A fruit dessert or other light fare is the best way to end an abundant meal. If the meal featured a vegetable main dish, such as stuffed peppers or cabbage rolls, a high-protein dessert would be best for filling the day's nutritional needs. So choose from a variety of smooth custards rich in egg and milk. And when the meal — be it lunch or dinner — has not included potatoes or other starches, why not serve a filling rice pudding?

The pressure cooker is a boon to the dessert cook, especially during the summer months when she wants to serve a custard or other baked dessert but hates to heat up her kitchen by using the oven. The custards and fluffy bread and rice puddings are so easily done in the pressure cooker and in so little time.

FRESH FRUIT DELIGHTS

**Apple, cut in half,
core removed
Cantaloupe, cut in half,
seeds removed**

**Nectarine
Peach
Pear
½ cup water**

Choose your favorites. Place water, cooking rack, and fruit in pressure cooker. Do not fill over ⅔ full. Close cover securely. Place pressure regulator on vent pipe. COOK 0 MINUTES. Cool pressure cooker at once. Serve immediately.

LEMON RICE DESSERT

**2 cups milk
2 eggs
½ cup sugar
½ teaspoon salt
2 teaspoons grated
lemon rind**

**1 cup cooked rice
¼ cup toasted slivered
almonds
½ cup water**

Scald milk; cool. Beat eggs, sugar, and salt together. Add milk, stirring constantly. Mix in lemon rind, rice, and almonds. Pour into custard cups; cover with aluminum foil. Place water, cooking rack, and custard cups in pressure cooker. Close cover securely. Place pressure regulator on vent pipe. COOK 3 MINUTES. Cool pressure cooker at once. 4 to 6 servings.

CHOCOLATE DROPS

**1 12-ounce package semi-
sweet chocolate chips
1 14-ounce can sweetened
condensed milk**

**1 cup raisins
4 cups water
1 cup chopped pecans**

Combine chocolate chips, condensed milk, and raisins; mix well. Pour into a bowl; cover with aluminum foil. Place water, cooking rack, and bowl in pressure cooker. Close cover securely. Place pressure regulator on vent pipe. COOK 8 MINUTES. Cool pressure cooker at once. Remove bowl; stir in nuts. Set bowl in cold water until mixture is cold. Drop by teaspoonfuls onto wax paper; let stand until firm. Yields approximately 4 dozen chocolate drops.

*It's a dessert but it would also
make a beautiful garnish for
a platter of turkey or ham
at holiday time.*

ORANGE CUPS

3 oranges
1 tablespoon sugar
1 cup seedless green
  grapes

2 tablespoons chopped
  pecans
6 maraschino cherries
½ cup water

Cut oranges in half crosswise. Remove orange sections;
place in a bowl. Reserve orange cups. Gently stir
together orange sections, sugar, grapes, and pecans.
Spoon mixture into orange cups. Top each with a
maraschino cherry. Place water, cooking rack, and filled
orange cups in pressure cooker. Close cover securely.
Place pressure regulator on vent pipe. COOK 0 MINUTES.
Cool pressure cooker at once. 6 servings.

Old-time fruit goodness.

PEACH BETTY

3 cups graham cracker crumbs
¼ cup melted butter
3 cups drained, sliced, canned peaches
½ cup water

3 tablespoons lemon juice
1 tablespoon grated lemon rind
¾ cup sugar
2 cups water

Moisten crumbs with butter. Place alternate layers of crumbs and peaches in buttered mold. Sprinkle each layer with mixture of ½ cup water, lemon juice, lemon rind, and sugar. Cover bowl with aluminum foil. Place 2 cups water, cooking rack, and mold in pressure cooker. Close cover securely. Place pressure regulator on vent pipe. COOK 8 MINUTES. Cool pressure cooker at once. 6 to 8 servings.

Variation: for Apple Betty, substitute sliced fresh apples for peaches. COOK 15 MINUTES.

CHEWY CHERRY DESSERT

1 20-ounce can sour cherries
1 cup white sugar
3 tablespoons flour

½ cup rolled oats
½ cup brown sugar
¼ cup melted butter
2 cups water

Drain juice from cherries. Set cherries aside. Blend white sugar with flour; add to juice. Cook until thickened, stirring constantly. Blend in cherries, rolled oats, brown sugar, and melted butter. Pour into a buttered mold. Do not fill over ⅔ full. Cover with aluminum foil. Place water, cooking rack, and mold in pressure cooker. Close cover securely. Place pressure regulator on vent pipe. COOK 15 MINUTES. Cool pressure cooker at once. Serve hot or cold. Top with whipped cream or ice cream, if desired. 6 servings.

Puddings can be cooked in an ordinary mixing bowl.
For that extra special touch, use a fluted or ring mold.

PEACH PUDDING

2 cups flour
3 teaspoons baking powder
½ teaspoon salt
1 cup sugar
4 tablespoons butter

2 eggs
1 cup milk
2 cups sliced canned peaches
5 cups water

Sift dry ingredients together; cut in butter. Beat eggs slightly, combine with milk; add to flour mixture. Add peaches and mix lightly. Pour into buttered mold. Do not fill mold over ⅔ full. Cover with aluminum foil. Place water, cooking rack, and mold in pressure cooker. Close cover securely. ALLOW STEAM TO FLOW FROM VENT PIPE FOR 15 MINUTES. Place pressure regulator on vent pipe. COOK 30 MINUTES. Cool pressure cooker at once. Remove foil; let pudding stand about 5 minutes before removing from bowl. Serve warm, with whipped cream, if desired. 6 to 8 servings.

A selection of company-best desserts is part of the Gourmet Meals section, pages 28 through 43.

Young health-food enthusiasts are discovering the dark, rich flavor of molasses as a sweetener. It's high in iron too.

PLANTATION CUSTARD

3 eggs, slightly beaten
¼ cup molasses
1 tablespoon sugar
¼ teaspoon salt

¾ teaspoon lemon extract
2 cups hot milk
½ cup water

Combine eggs, molasses, sugar, salt, and lemon extract. Stir in hot milk. Pour into custard cups; cover with aluminum foil. Place water, cooking rack, and custard cups in pressure cooker. Close cover securely. Place pressure regulator on vent pipe. COOK 3 MINUTES. Cool pressure cooker at once. 4 to 6 servings.

*Here is a way to enjoy the
sweet-spicy flavor of pumpkin
pie without the high-calorie
pastry.*

PUMPKIN CUSTARD PUDDING

1 cup milk
2 eggs, beaten
1¼ cups cooked
   mashed pumpkin
⅓ teaspoon salt
½ cup brown sugar

1½ tablespoons sugar
1 teaspoon cinnamon
⅓ teaspoon ginger
¼ teaspoon ground cloves
½ cup water

Combine all ingredients, except water; beat until
well blended. Pour into custard cups; cover with
aluminum foil. Place water, cooking rack, and custard
cups in pressure cooker. Close cover securely.
Place pressure regulator on vent pipe. COOK 10
MINUTES. Cool pressure cooker at once. Serve warm
or chilled. Garnish with whipped cream and nuts,
if desired. 4 to 6 servings.

SUGAR FREE VANILLA CUSTARD

1 cup skim milk
1 egg
   Artificial sweetener to
   equal 3 tablespoons sugar

½ teaspoon vanilla
½ cup water

Scald milk; cool. Beat egg and artificial sweetener. Add
milk, stirring constantly. Mix in vanilla. Pour into custard
cups; cover with aluminum foil. Place water, cooking rack,
and custard cups in pressure cooker. Close cover securely.
Place pressure regulator on vent pipe. COOK 3 MINUTES.
Cool pressure cooker at once. 2 to 3 servings.

Variations:
Coffee Custard: Substitute 1½ teaspoons instant coffee
for vanilla. Dissolve instant coffee in scalded milk.

Almond Custard: Substitute ½ teaspoon almond extract
for vanilla.

PEPPERMINT NUT CUSTARD

2 cups milk
½ cup crushed peppermint
  stick candy
2 eggs, beaten

¼ teaspoon salt
½ teaspoon vanilla
½ cup water
¼ cup chopped walnuts

Scald milk. Dissolve candy in milk; cool slightly.
Combine eggs, salt, and vanilla. Add milk, stirring
constantly. Pour into custard cups. Cover with
aluminum foil. Place water, cooking rack, and custard
cups in pressure cooker. Close cover securely. Place
pressure regulator on vent pipe. COOK 3 MINUTES.
Cool pressure cooker at once. Chill. Unmold;
sprinkle with walnuts. 4 to 6 servings.

*Treat your family to homemade
chocolate pudding. It's so easy
to make in the pressure cooker.*

CHOCOLATE PUDDING

3 tablespoons butter
¾ cup sugar
1 egg, beaten
2¼ cups flour
2 tablespoons baking
  powder

¼ teaspoon salt
4 tablespoons cocoa
1 cup milk
5 cups water

Cream butter and sugar; add egg. Sift dry ingredients
together; add alternately with milk. Pour into
buttered mold. Do not fill mold over ⅔ full. Cover with
aluminum foil. Place water, cooking rack, and mold in
pressure cooker. Close cover securely. ALLOW STEAM
TO FLOW FROM VENT PIPE FOR 15 MINUTES. Place
pressure regulator on vent pipe. COOK 25 MINUTES.
Let pressure drop of its own accord.

*It's fun to have a variety of dishes for serving dessert. Pick up
an extra set at a garage sale or auction. Or collect antique
dessert dishes, all different, as some collect cups and saucers.*

DESSERTS

*Americans, especially
Midwesterners, are chocolate
lovers of long standing.
From hot cocoa through
fudge cake to a creamy
pudding like this, make
ours chocolate.*

CHOCOLATE CUSTARD

2½ cups milk	1 teaspoon vanilla
3 eggs	½ cup chocolate chips
½ cup sugar	1 tablespoon butter
½ teaspoon salt	½ cup water

Scald milk; cool. Beat eggs, sugar, salt, and vanilla;
add milk, mixing briskly. Melt chocolate chips
and butter. Stir egg mixture into melted chocolate.
Pour into custard cups; cover with aluminum foil.
Place water, cooking rack, and custard cups in pressure
cooker. Close cover securely. Place pressure regulator
on vent pipe. COOK 3 MINUTES. Cool pressure cooker
at once. Chill custards. 4 to 6 servings.

Variations:
Mocha Custard: Dissolve 1½ teaspoons instant
coffee in scalded milk.
Chocolate Rum Custard: Subsitute 1 tablespoon rum or
1 teaspoon rum extract for vanilla.

OLD-FASHIONED CARAMEL CUSTARD

2 cups milk	4 eggs, slightly beaten
1 cup dark corn syrup	1 teaspoon vanilla
½ teaspoon salt	½ cup water

Scald milk; add corn syrup and salt. Pour milk mixture
into beaten eggs, stirring constantly. Add vanilla.
Pour into custard cups; cover with aluminum foil.
Place water, cooking rack, and custard cups in pressure
cooker. Close cover securely. Place pressure regulator
on vent pipe. COOK 3 MINUTES. Cool pressure cooker
at once. 4 to 6 servings.

HAWAIIAN RICE PUDDING

1½ cups milk
  2 eggs, slightly beaten
⅓ cup brown sugar
½ teaspoon salt
½ cup cooked rice

1 13½-ounce can crushed
    pineapple, drained
½ cup slivered almonds
½ cup water

Scald milk; cool slightly. Combine eggs, sugar, and salt. Add milk, stirring constantly. Add rice, pineapple, and almonds. Pour into individual custard cups and cover with aluminum foil. Place water, cooking rack, and custard cups in pressure cooker. Close cover securely. Place pressure regulator on vent pipe. COOK 3 MINUTES. Cool pressure cooker at once. Chill. Unmold, if desired. 4 to 6 servings.

*Serve with Sopaipillas, a wedge-
shaped Spanish dough deep
fried until puffed and golden.*

BIZCOCHO CON GRENADINA SAUCE

3 pears, peeled and cut into quarters	6 slices sponge cake
½ cup grenadine syrup	1 tablespoon cornstarch
	⅓ cup water

Place pear quarters in pressure cooker. Pour grenadine
syrup over pears. Close cover securely. Place pressure
regulator on vent pipe. COOK 0 MINUTES. Cool
pressure cooker at once. Place two pear quarters on
each slice of cake. Blend cornstarch with water. Add
to syrup in pressure cooker. Heat until sauce is clear and
thickened, stirring constantly. Pour sauce over pears
and cake. Garnish with slivered almonds, if desired.
Serve either warm or chilled. 4 to 6 servings.

PINEAPPLE BREAD PUDDING

5 slices day-old bread	5 cups water
1 cup crushed pineapple	½ cup pineapple juice
2 eggs	2 tablespoons brown sugar
¼ cup sugar	2 teaspoons cornstarch
2 cups hot milk	¼ cup coarsely chopped pecans
¼ teaspoon cinnamon	

Remove crusts; cut bread slices into 1-inch strips.
In a buttered mold, place alternate layers of bread and
pineapple. Beat eggs; stir in sugar and milk. Pour
mixture over bread and pineapple leaving 1 inch
expansion space. Sprinkle cinnamon over top. Cover
with aluminum foil. Place water, cooking rack, and
mold in pressure cooker. Close cover securely.
ALLOW STEAM TO FLOW FROM VENT PIPE FOR
5 MINUTES. Place pressure regulator on vent pipe.
COOK 10 MINUTES. Let pressure drop of its own
accord. Unmold pudding.

Combine pineapple juice, brown sugar, and cornstarch
in a saucepan. Cook over low heat, stirring to blend.
Drizzle sauce over pudding. Sprinkle with pecans.
6 to 8 servings.

*This dessert is wholesome
when made with white bread,
hearty and old-fashioned when
made with whole wheat.*

TAFFY BREAD PUDDING

2 eggs, slightly beaten
¼ cup molasses
1 tablespoon sugar
¼ teaspoon salt

¼ teaspoon nutmeg
1 cup soft bread cubes
1½ cups hot milk
½ cup water

Combine eggs, molasses, sugar, salt, and nutmeg. Add
bread cubes. Stir in hot milk. Pour into custard cups;
cover with aluminum foil. Place water, cooking rack,
and custard cups in pressure cooker. Close cover
securely. Place pressure regulator on vent pipe.
COOK 3 MINUTES. Cool pressure cooker at once.
4 to 6 servings.

FRUITED BREAD PUDDING

2 eggs, beaten
½ teaspoon vanilla
½ cup sugar
¼ teaspoon salt
½ teaspoon cinnamon
4 slices white bread,
cubed

1½ cups hot milk
1 8-ounce can fruit
cocktail, drained
4 cups water

Combine eggs, vanilla, sugar, salt, and cinnamon. Add
bread cubes. Stir in hot milk and fruit cocktail. Pour into
a buttered mold. Do not fill over ⅔ full. Cover mold with
aluminum foil. Place water, cooking rack, and mold in
pressure cooker. Close cover securely. Place pressure
regulator on vent pipe. COOK 15 MINUTES. Let pressure
drop of its own accord. Serve hot or cold, with hard
sauce or ice cream, if desired. 4 to 6 servings.

BRAZILIAN RAISIN SAUCE WITH BANANAS

½ **cup seedless raisins**
¾ **cup pineapple juice**
4 **tablespoons honey**
⅛ **teaspoon salt**
1 **teaspoon cornstarch**

1 **tablespoon water**
1 **tablespoon butter**
6 **large ripe bananas,**
sliced lengthwise

Place first four ingredients in pressure cooker. Close
cover securely. Place pressure regulator on vent pipe.
COOK 3 MINUTES. Cool pressure cooker at once.
Dissolve cornstarch in water. Add to sauce in
pressure cooker; cook until thickened. Stir in butter.
Chill sauce. Pour over bananas. Garnish with
shredded coconut, if desired. 6 servings.

A pressure-cooked version of the popular fruit soup which Scandinavians serve hot or cold for breakfast or dessert. For some, a bowl of this hot fruit with toast is a favorite Saturday lunch.

DRIED FRUIT COMPOTE

1 12-ounce package
  mixed dried fruits
2 cups orange juice
3 tablespoons lemon juice
2 tablespoons sugar

Rind of 1 orange, cut
  into strips
Rind of 1 lemon, cut
  into strips

Combine all ingredients in pressure cooker. Close cover securely. Place pressure regulator on vent pipe. COOK 5 MINUTES. Cool pressure cooker at once. Chill. If desired, garnish with whipped cream.

Variation: Substitute a favorite individual dried fruit for the mixed dried fruits.

If fruit is very dry, soak overnight in orange juice in a covered dish.

SWEDISH FRUIT SOUP

4 cups mixed fresh fruit,
  cut into pieces
½ cup water

½ lemon, sliced
¼ cup sugar
¼ teaspoon cinnamon

Combine fruit, water, lemon, sugar, and cinnamon in pressure cooker. Close cover securely. Place pressure regulator on vent pipe. COOK 0 MINUTES. Cool pressure cooker at once. If desired, thicken with cornstarch or arrowroot. 4 to 6 servings.

Peaches, pears, nectarines, and oranges are especially good this way.

MORE TREASURES

A potpourri of miscellany? Here is a chapter for a variety of recipes that did not command a section of their own but were simply too good to relegate to the round file.

There are relishes for the gardener-canner and appetizers for the party-giver. There are treats — popcorn and fudge — which the smart mom can use to introduce pressure cooking to her upcoming cooks — male and female.

Perhaps we should have called them "Last but not Least"? Or, better yet, "More Pleasures," for, to many a cook, the discovery of a new recipe or a new method (like turning a can of milk into a dessert sauce without ever opening the can) is a distinct pleasure.

An attractive do-ahead appetizer that is not as high in calories as some.

TANGY COCKTAIL MUSHOOMS

3 lbs. mushrooms
6 cloves garlic, diced
1 tablespoon olive oil
½ teaspoon oregano

⅛ teaspoon crushed red hot pepper
1 tablespoon Marsala wine
¼ cup water

Combine all ingredients in pressure cooker. Close cover securely. Place pressure regulator on vent pipe. COOK 0 MINUTES. Cool pressure cooker at once. Chill mushrooms. Serve with cocktail picks.

Variation: Substitute vinegar for Marsala wine.

MARINATED CARROTS

¼ cup cooking oil
2 cloves garlic, minced
1 onion, chopped
2 lbs. carrots, sliced ¼-inch thick

1½ tablespoons whole pickling spice
2 teaspoons salt
1 teaspoon dry mustard
⅛ teaspoon pepper
⅓ cup vinegar

Heat pressure cooker. Add oil; sauté garlic and onion. Add remaining ingredients. Close cover securely. Place pressure regulator on vent pipe. COOK 2 MINUTES. Cool pressure cooker at once. Chill. Drain and serve as relish.

OYSTER-STUFFED CHERRY TOMATOES

1 pint fresh oysters, drained

½ cup water
1 pint cherry tomatoes

Place oysters on cooking rack in pressure cooker; add water. Close cover securely. Place pressure regulator on vent pipe. COOK 2 MINUTES. Cool pressure cooker at once. Cut a slit in each cherry tomato; fill with oysters. Cut very large oysters into two or three pieces. Serve appetizers on wooden or plastic picks.

Shrimp — something to splurge on and then enjoy — makes your party special.

PICKLED SHRIMP

2 lbs. frozen shrimp, deveined
¼ cup cooking oil
½ cup lime juice
2 tablespoons wine vinegar

1 tablespoon chopped chives
1½ teaspoons salt
½ teaspoon dried dill seed
3 drops Tabasco sauce

Place shrimp in pressure cooker. Combine remaining ingredients; pour over shrimp. Close cover securely. Place pressure regulator on vent pipe. COOK 0 MINUTES. Let pressure drop of its own accord. Chill. Drain; serve with cocktail picks.

Looking for another tidbit for an open house or cocktail party? Here's one that is high in flavor without high cost.

'LOBSTER' CANAPES

1 recipe Poor Man's 'Lobster' (page 114)
½ cup canned condensed cream of mushroom soup
2 tablespoons cooking sherry

1 tablespoon chopped pimiento
¼ teaspoon salt
2 drops Tabasco sauce
2½ dozen toasted bread rounds

Combine 'lobster', mushroom soup, sherry, pimiento, salt and Tabasco sauce. Spread on bread rounds.

*For your next party, skip
the marinated herring and
serve this.*

DEVILED SOLE APPETIZERS

1 lb. sole fillets	1½ teaspoon
Salt and pepper	Worcestershire sauce
¼ cup hot water	½ teaspoon dry mustard
1 teaspoon instant	½ teaspoon paprika
chicken bouillon	½ teaspoon parsley flakes

Sprinkle sole fillets with salt and pepper. Place fillets in
pressure cooker. Combine remaining ingredients;
pour over fillets. Close cover securely. Place pressure
regulator on vent pipe. COOK 5 MINUTES. Let
pressure drop of its own accord. Drain sole fillets on
absorbent paper and chill. Cut into bite size pieces;
serve on picks.

SPANISH FRUIT APPETIZER

2 oranges, peeled and sectioned	½ cup Maderia wine
	½ cup sugar
2 pink grapefruit, peeled and sectioned	2 tablespoons cornstarch
	¼ cup water
3 pears, peeled and cut into quarters	

Place fruit in pressure cooker. Blend Maderia wine and
sugar; pour over fruit. Close cover securely. Place
pressure regulator on vent pipe. COOK 0 MINUTES.
Cool pressure cooker at once. Remove fruit from
pressure cooker. Blend cornstarch with water; add to
sauce in pressure cooker. Heat, stirring constantly
until thickened. Spoon sauce over fruit. Garnish with
slivered almonds, if desired. 4 to 6 servings.

Quick, iron-rich . . .
for breakfast.

PRESSURE-COOKED PRUNES

1 cup prunes
1 cup pineapple juice

Place prunes and pineapple juice in pressure cooker.
Close cover securely. Place pressure regulator on
vent pipe. COOK 5 MINUTES. Cool pressure cooker
at once. Chill prunes.

Variation: Use apple cider or orange juice in place
of pineapple juice.

If prunes are very dry, soak in juice overnight in a
covered dish before cooking.

Here is a quick and easy way
to hard-cook 10 or 12 eggs
at once for deviled eggs or a
picnic salad. Remember that
very fresh eggs are harder to
peel after hard-cooking than
eggs several days old.

HARD-COOKED EGGS

Place 1 cup water, cooking rack, and eggs in pressure
cooker. Close cover securely. Place pressure regulator
on vent pipe. COOK 6 MINUTES. Cool pressure cooker
at once.

PRESSURE-POACHED EGGS

Grease custard cups well; break one egg into each cup.
Season eggs with salt and pepper. Place 1 cup water,
cooking rack, and custard cups in pressure cooker.
Close cover securely. Place pressure regulator on vent
pipe. COOK 1½ MINUTES. Cool pressure cooker at once.

GARLIC BEANS

1 lb. whole green beans
1 onion, sliced
1 clove garlic, minced
¼ cup sugar

½ cup white wine vinegar
1 tablespoon olive oil
½ teaspoon salt

Combine all ingredients in pressure cooker. Close
cover securely. Place pressure regulator on vent pipe.
COOK 4 MINUTES. Cool pressure cooker at once.
Chill beans. Drain and serve as relish.

*Washing the mushrooms
individually is the hardest part
of preparing this appetizer.*

PICKLED MUSHROOMS

2 lbs. mushrooms
¼ cup olive oil
⅓ cup wine vinegar
1½ teaspoons salt
1 teaspoon sugar

½ teaspoon basil
8 peppercorns
1 bay leaf
1 clove garlic, minced

Place all ingredients in pressure cooker. Close cover
securely. Place pressure regulator on vent pipe.
COOK 0 MINUTES. Cool pressure cooker at once.
Chill. Drain and serve as relish.

CRACKING NUTS

Place 1 cup water, cooking rack, and unshelled nuts in
pressure cooker. Do not fill pressure cooker over
⅔ full. Close cover securely. Place pressure
regulator on vent pipe. COOK 5 TO 6 MINUTES
for Brazil or any hard thick shelled nuts. Reduce time
for thinner shelled nuts. Cool pressure cooker at once.
A light tap with a hammer will open the shells and the
nut meats may be removed whole. If nuts are moist,
place in a warm oven, for a few minutes, to dry.

Roasted Nuts

*Mix 1 teaspoon cooking oil with 1 cup shelled nuts.
Spread in a shallow pan. Roast at 350° for 15 minutes
or until lightly browned, stirring occasionally.
Sprinkle the hot nuts with salt.*

FUDGE

1 14-ounce can sweetened
  condensed milk
2 6-ounce packages
  chocolate chips

1 cup chopped walnuts
1 teaspoon vanilla
  (optional)
2 cups water

Combine milk and chocolate chips in a bowl that will
fit loosely in pressure cooker. Cover bowl with
aluminum foil. Place water, cooking rack, and bowl in
pressure cooker. Close cover securely. Place pressure
regulator on vent pipe. COOK 5 MINUTES. Cool
pressure cooker at once. Remove bowl. Stir mixture
until evenly blended. Do not beat. Add nuts and
vanilla. Blend until mixture is smooth. Turn into cool
bowl and let stand without beating until fudge is cold.
Drop by teaspoons onto waxed paper.

CARAMELIZED DESSERT TOPPING

Place 4 cups water, cooking rack, and a 14-ounce can
of sweetened condensed milk in pressure cooker.
Close cover securely. Place pressure regulator on vent
pipe. COOK 60 MINUTES. Let pressure drop of its
own accord. Serve over fruit or cake, if desired.

POPCORN

⅓ cup unsalted cooking oil   **½ cup popcorn**

Place oil and popcorn in pressure cooker. Remove sealing ring from cover, as dry heat tends to deteriorate sealing ring. Place cover on pressure cooker. Do not use pressure regulator. Set heat on high. When corn starts to pop reduce heat. As soon as corn stops popping, pour into large bowl. Add salt and melted butter, if desired.

Between successive batches, wipe pressure cooker with a paper towel and proceed as above.

If corn does not pop satisfactorily, it is usually an indication that the corn is too dry. Store opened containers of popcorn in refrigerator to restore moisture.

Look for fruit with perfect, unblemished skins for they make the most attractive marmalade. A jar of your own marmalade makes the ideal, thoughtful gift.

CITRUS MARMALADE

2 cups thinly sliced
oranges
¼ cup thinly sliced lemon

3½ cups water
3¼ cups sugar

Cut orange and lemon slices into quarters. Place fruit and water in pressure cooker. Close cover securely. Place pressure regulator on vent pipe. COOK 3 MINUTES. Cool pressure cooker at once. Stir in sugar. Boil, without cover, stirring occasionally until mixture reaches jell stage. Pour into sterilized jelly glasses. Seal and label.

A conserve has nuts in it . . . a preserve does not.

PEACH CONSERVE

1 small unpeeled orange,
chopped
6 large peaches, peeled
and sliced
½ cup water

2½ cups sugar
¼ teaspoon ground
ginger
½ cup slivered almonds

Place orange, peaches and water in pressure cooker. Close cover securely. Place pressure regulator on vent pipe. COOK 5 MINUTES. Cool pressure cooker at once. Stir in sugar and ginger. Boil, without cover, stirring occasionally until mixture reaches jell stage. Add almonds and heat through. Pour into hot sterilized glasses. Seal and label.

It's wise to prepare and seal jars with care. Consult a reliable souce, such as U.S. Dept. of Agriculture Extension Service or the Kerr or Ball canning jar companies, for complete information on preparing and sealing jars of conserves and marmalades.

Candied peel is delicious eaten
"as is" as a sweet. Or use it
in foods like fruitcake.

CANDIED ORANGE AND GRAPEFRUIT PEEL

3 oranges	4 cups sugar
3 grapefruit	2 cups water
1 cup water	. . . . .
. . . . .	½ cup sugar

Cut each orange and grapefruit into quarters lengthwise.
Remove pulp with a spoon. Place 1 cup water and peel
in pressure cooker. Close cover securely. Place
pressure regulator on vent pipe. COOK 6 MINUTES.
Cool pressure cooker at once. Drain peel and remove
white membrane. Cut peel into ½-inch strips.
Return peel to pressure cooker. Add 4 cups sugar and
2 cups water. Close cover securely. Place pressure
regulator on vent pipe. COOK 1 MINUTE. Let pressure
drop of its own accord. Drain peel, dry on absorbent
paper. Roll peel in ½ cup sugar. Dry thoroughly on a
wire rack. For best results, dry in oven at very low
temperature. It will take a couple of hours for peel
to crisp.

READY PUMPKIN

Cut a pumpkin in half. Scoop out seeds and pulp.
Cut halves into two-inch wedges and peel. Cut wedges
in half. Place 1 cup water, cooking rack, and pumpkin
in pressure cooker. Do not fill over ⅔ full. Close cover
securely. Place pressure regulator on vent pipe.
COOK 10 MINUTES. Cool pressure cooker at once.
Mash pumpkin, beat with an electric mixer, or puree in
a blender. Use in a favorite pumpkin pie or nut bread
recipe! Or freeze, for future use.

HINTS AND HELPS
For Using Your Pressure Cooker

Be sure to thoroughly read and carefully follow all directions by the manufacturer of your pressure cooker.

WHEN FOOD STICKS OR GETS DARK IN COOKER

It is disappointing and frustrating to open the cooker and find that your food has stuck to the bottom or has nearly burned. There may be several reasons for this happening. Perhaps you are hurrying the cooking and have the heat too high when building up the pressure. Perhaps you have used too much flour in coating meat and it has stuck in browning. Perhaps you have not used enough liquid for your cooking. It is best to use recipes tested in the cooker, like those in this book, until you become adept at pressure cooking.

MOLDS — GLASS, METAL OR EARTHENWARE

This book includes a variety of recipes for foods cooked in molds: custards, vegetable ramekin, and molded seafood. As molds you can use glass custard cups, the 4- or 6-ounce size, metal or tin gelatin molds or little earthernware souffle dishes. The molds must fit loosely in the pressure cooker.

Fill molds up to ⅔ full to allow for expansion of food during cooking. Molds and custard cups can be covered with aluminum foil or several layers of waxed paper securely tied with clean white string.

RACK — FOR TWO LAYERS OF MOLDS

Because molds filled with food to be pressure cooked should be arranged so that steam circulates freely, it is smart to use a second cooking rack. It's easy to arrange 3 custard cups or 4 molds on the rack that came with your cooker, then a second rack and a second layer of molds.

A second rack may be ordered from your cooker manufacturer for a small fee or purchased at the hardware store or one may be fashioned from a disposable round aluminum pan — just pierce holes in the bottom of the pan with tines of fork or point of knife.

ADDITIONAL SUGGESTIONS

Before pressure cooking, sear meat well to seal in juices. To prevent meat from sticking, preheat pan, add shortening and sear meat.

During cooking, some foods have a tendency to foam, froth, sputter and may block necessary openings in the pressure cooker cover. Therefore, do not pressure cook apple sauce, cranberries, rhubarb, pearl barley, split peas, cereals or foods such as noodles, macaroni or spaghetti.

HOW TO ADAPT FAVORITE RECIPES
TO PRESSURE COOKING

Once you have become skilled in the use of your pressure cooker, you will want to adapt some of your favorite recipes to pressure cooking.

Spending a few minutes in converting a pet recipe will pay dividends in time saved as you use the recipe over and over. Just jot down the amount of liquid, pressure cooking time and method of cooling the cooker on the recipe card or book page.

Recipes for soups, meat, poultry, seafood, vegetables and many combination foods can easily be adapted to pressure cooking. Here are the three important things to determine and check:

1) Amount of liquid. Use comparable recipes in this book as your guide. In general, when preparing soups and braised meats, the amount of water can be reduced from the traditional recipe because it allows for water evaporation during the long cooking. Vegetables contain a high percentage of water, some of which will be released during cooking. Therefore, vegetables and mixtures including vegetables may need only small amounts of water. At least ½ cup water is always added to the cooker for the production of steam.

2) Cooking time. The length of time that a food should be pressure cooked is usually one-third (⅓) of the cooking time given in your recipe. Do not start counting time until 15 lbs. pressure has been reached and you have lowered heat for cooking.

3) Method of cooling the cooker. Whether you should cool the cooker immediately or let pressure drop of its own accord depends on the type of food being prepared. Again, checking a similar recipe in this book is helpful. In general, large solid pieces of meat, like roasts, should continue to cook while pressure drops by itself. For most other foods, the cooker can be cooled right away and food served immediately.

Use of the rack is another thing to decide upon in adapting personal recipes to the pressure cooker. When you want a blending of flavors during cooking, place food in the cooking liquid (water, broth, beer, etc.). When you wish to cook foods such as roasts out of the liquid, place them on the rack, above the liquid.

Some cooks like a crisper exterior on their meats than is usually produced by the pressure cooker. For a crisp outside, just broil meat a minute or two after removing from the cooker.

In high altitude areas, cooking time should be increased 5% for every 1000 feet above the first 2000 feet.

Knowing How To Do It Can Make Cleaning Your Pressure Cooker a Pleasure

OUTSIDE

Keep the exterior of your pressure cooker bright and shiny by simply washing it with soap and water. If some stains are a bit stubborn, use a nylon mesh scouring pad. Do not use steel wool pads or abrasive kitchen cleansers.

INSIDE

The cooker will wash clean in a moment if it is filled with warm water as soon as food is removed and soaked during mealtime. The inside of your cooker, whether it is the popular aluminum or stainless steel, may discolor due to minerals in water and foods. Consult the instruction booklet furnished with your cooker by the manufacturer to learn how to remove any discoloration.

SEALING RING

First, remove the sealing ring from the cooker cover. Then, using a small brush, scrub the cover grooves. Finally, wash the ring and replace it. This should be done periodically, every few months at least.

VENT PIPE

It is very important to keep the cooker's vent pipe open because the air must be exhausted from the cooker before the steam cooking can begin. Clean the vent pipe quickly and easily by thrusting a pipe cleaner through it. Never use a toothpick or anything else which could break off and become lodged in the vent pipe. A clogged vent pipe will interfere with the adjustment of pressure during cooking.

DISHWASHER

If you wish to wash the cooker in your dishwasher, always remove the sealing ring and automatic air vent before placing the cooker in the dishwasher. This is to prevent the high heat of the drying cycle from damaging these critical parts of the cooker. Submersible electric cookers may also be washed in the dishwasher. Many homemakers, however, prefer to wash their cookers by hand rather than fill up to ¼ of one level of their dishwasher with one utensil.

PARTS OF A TYPICAL PRESSURE COOKER

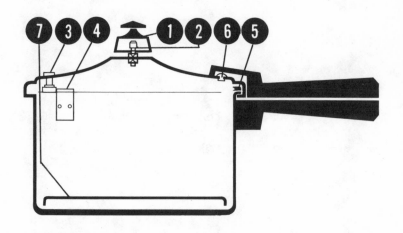

1. **PRESSURE REGULATOR** — gauge which indicates and regulates the steam pressure. Fifteen pounds pressure is ideal for cooking foods.

2. **VENT PIPE** — projecting tube on the cover which holds the pressure regulator and allows steam to escape.

3. **AIR VENT/COVER LOCK** — exhausts air from the pressure cooker before pressure is built up. Also acts as a visual indication of pressure in the pressure cooker.

4. **LOCKING BRACKET** — located on the inside of the pressure cooker body, engages with the air vent/cover lock to prevent the cover from being opened when there is pressure in the unit.

5. **SEALING RING** — gasket made of a rubber-like material which fits into the cover and forms a pressure-tight seal for cooking.

6. **OVERPRESSURE PLUG** — located under the cover handle, it automatically releases steam in case the vent pipe becomes clogged and pressure cannot be released normally.

7. **COOKING RACK** — a perforated rack placed into the pressure cooker body for cooking foods out of water.

TABLE OF EQUIVALENTS

In planning your meals and writing your grocery lists, you often need to translate the measurements called for in the recipes to the weights and measures the ingredients are sold by. This list of common ingredients, many of them called for in this book, should be helpful in being a smart grocery shopper.

FRESH VEGETABLES
Beets: 1 lb. (med.) = 2 cups, chopped
Cabbage: 1 lb. = 4 cups, shredded
Carrots: 1 lb. (8 small) = 4 cups, chopped
Celery: 1 stalk = ½ cup, finely chopped
Corn: 6 ears = 1½ cups, cut
Cucumber: 1 med. = 1½ cups, sliced
Mushrooms: ½ lb. (20 med.) = 2 cups, sliced
Onions: 1 med. = 1 cup, finely chopped
Peas, in pods: 1 lb. = 1 cup, shelled
Potatoes: 1 lb. (4 med.) = 2½ cups, cooked and diced
Spinach, fresh: 1 lb. = 8 cups, fresh; 2 cups, cooked
Tomatoes: 1 lb. (3 med.) = 1¼ cups, chopped

DRIED VEGETABLES
Rice: 1 lb. (2½ cups) = 8 cups, cooked
Kidney beans: 1 lb. (1½ cups) = 9 cups, cooked
Lima or navy beans: 1 lb. (2½ cups) = 6 cups, cooked

FRESH FRUITS
Apples: 1 lb. (4 small) = 3 cups, chopped
Bananas: 1 lb. (4 small) = 2 cups, mashed
Lemon: 1 med. = 3 tbsp. juice
Orange: 1 small = 2 tsp. grated peel; 6 tbsp. juice

MEAT AND CHEESE
Beef, cooked: 1 lb. = 4 cups, chopped
Beef, raw, ground: 1 lb. = 2 cups
Beef, raw, roast: 1 lb. = ¾ lbs., cooked
Beef or chicken stock base, powdered: 1 tsp. = 1 bouillon cube
Cheese, grated: ¼ lb. = 1 cup

HERBS AND SEASONINGS
Garlic: 1 small clove = ⅛ tsp. garlic powder
Herbs: ½ tsp. dried = 1 tbsp. fresh

INDEX

INDEX

INDEX